Pr

MY DAYS

MW00810606

"Paul Dunion's *My Days with Emma: A Soulful Path to Elderhood* is not only a wise book; it is a practical guide to the reconfiguring of one's life. He covers the questions, the resistances, and the developmental tasks of aging as well as anyone I know. His conversations with Emma, a wise woman senior to him, is both an outer encounter with a woman who has lived the journey and reflected on it, and an inner encounter with his own questioning, anxious, yet resourceful anima. This book is especially practical for men because it asks questions for them that rest still unspoken in their hearts, and for women who want to know more about those strange creatures we call men."

> – **James Hollis, PhD, Jungian Analyst; Author,** *The Broken Mirror: Refracted Visions of Ourselves*

"In his latest book, *My Days with Emma: A Soulful Path to Elderhood*, Dr. Paul Dunion offers us a moving and incredibly soulful accounting of the vulnerability of aging and the profound movement into elderhood. He shares with raw candor his own inner exploration of the themes of mortality, physical frailty, and the poignant terrain of the initiatory journey and the maturation process of befriending Mystery.

"The book pivots around amazing soaring dialogues between Paul and his mentor Emma that provoke reflection and illumine the important life questions, thresholds, and lessons of this final third of life we are all marching toward. Whether you are young, in midlife, or entering eldership, these pages will lift you up, challenge you and help you to navigate your inner life going forward."

> – **Amy Elizabeth Fox, Chief Executive Officer, Mobius Executive Leadership**

"Beyond the "Golden Watch" awaits the rich opportunity to live deeply into the questions that guide a soulful life. In *My Days with Emma: A Soulful Path to Elderhood*, Dunion heart-fully unites the confluence of heart, maturity and wisdom into a rich inquiry and insight, illuminating a soulful path to elderhood. This book will serve anyone seeking a model and inspiration to age with grace while embracing the unique meanings offered in the second half of life."

> – **Jody Grose, Founder, Return to the Fire**

"Paul Dunion sees with eyes and writes with a voice of a modern-day mystic. This important text offers us a map of how to live with more curiosity, generosity, and gratitude as we move into the life stage Paul calls "eldership." One of the gifts of embracing our aging, he reminds us, is becoming more of who we authentically are rather than reducing life to what is practical, protective, and popular. Paul's stories have much to teach us about what it means to live a truly soulful life."

> – **Thom Allena, PhD, Instructor, Peace and Global Justice Studies Program - University of New Mexico; Co-Author, *Restorative Justice on the College Campus***

"I have known Paul Dunion for over 50 years, from crazy teens to Elderhood, a place we both currently occupy. In his latest book, *My Days with Emma: A Soulful Path to Elderhood*, I have found he has remained true to who he is - a soulful, compassionate, and intuitive author and individual. Within the pages of Emma, Paul eloquently leads the reader to find their own way to Elderhood."

> – **Bill Marshall, Author, *Pushing Against the Tide***

"In Paul Dunion's latest book, *My Days with Emma: A Soulful Path to Elderhood,* I came across this sentence that I am called to contemplate: 'It didn't take long for me to figure out that being an elder was mostly an offering to give to myself. Unlike being a teacher, apprenticing to elderhood seems to point away from something outside the self for validation.' This quiet yet powerful insight reflects the presence, the awakening of the inner elder. The elder within awaits our awareness of them, stepping willingly from within the curtains of time to be met with the wisdom of our awareness of them. The elders, these ancestors, are us. *My Days with Emma: A Soulful Path to Elderhood* is a useful map that helps us see the footprints on this soulful path and how we might, however awkwardly, learn to walk that journey."

> **– Ray DiCapua, Artist, Professor of Art, University of Connecticut**

MY DAYS WITH EMMA

A Soulful Path to Elderhood

Paul Dunion EdD

atmosphere press

Other Works by Paul Dunion

Wisdom: Apprenticing to the Unknown and Befriending Fate (2021)

Seekers: Finding Our Way Home (2016)

Path of the Novice Mystic:
Maintaining a Beginner's Heart and Mind (2014)

Dare to Grow Up: Learn to Become Who You Are Meant to Be
(2012)

Shadow Marriage: A Descent into Intimacy (2006)

Temptation in the House of the Lord (2004)

Dedicated to Norcott Pemberton
(*Emma*)

who walks with me during the depths of disillusionment
and defeat as well as in the delight of triumph.
She continuously celebrates stories of my gifts
finding their way into the world, greatly deepening
my devotion to serve in the winter of my life.

TABLE OF CONTENTS

PROLOGUE

The birth of this book took place when I was a nineteen-year-old student of philosophy, enthralled by the curiosities of so many who came before me. However, it wasn't until my friend Ray and I leaned into the topic of our aging during one of our regular coffee meetings that the knots unraveled in this book were first tied. We had addressed the topic previously, but for some reason, it demanded more airtime—perhaps because we each had recently been given a diagnosis that brought us closer to the non-permanence of life's journey. Despite having been diagnosed with Ménière's disease in March of 2018, it wasn't until April of 2020 that I realized the severity of my ailment.

I had looked away from my computer screen as the world started spinning, surrounding me in a vortex of vertigo. I then dropped to the floor and, with my wife's assistance, managed to flop onto a couch some six feet away, where I laid for five hours, retching and vomiting and unable to move. I finally crawled on my stomach to the bedroom, barely able to lift my head. That began a year and a half of bouts with dizziness and vertigo. In times of remission, I would find myself easily deluded into believing that I was on the other side of this debilitating malady, only to be cruelly reminded of its lingering presence.

It was too easy to slide into just needing this problem to

go away so I could get back to life as I knew it. I finally realized that many folks had the same attitude about the pandemic, a reaction I felt critical of and became uncomfortable reproducing as I faced my challenge. I began to understand that the wish for Ménière's to just go away meant I saw it as merely unfortunate. That attitude meant that the condition had nothing meaningful to offer me and that I could only be its victim. I wanted more.

I asked the question, "What is this condition of mine asking for?" I realized that the disorder was mostly compromising my balance. Should I be looking at balance in a larger way? Were there other ways in which my life was out of balance? I noticed that I lived with excessive severity and imbalance when it came to making room for joy and lightness. I was out of balance with regard to striving for improvement and accepting who I was. I was off balance when it came to allowing myself to taste life rather than attempt to figure it out.

Yes, many opportunities for tasting life had passed me by. During moments when I saw love and unbridled acceptance in someone's eyes being offered to me, I would feel tension and step away. I saw that so much of my life was about running toward something or away from something. I was way off balance regarding moving and pausing. It was hard to admit that I may have been a stranger to sweetness. I allowed myself to recognize sweetness but not taste it. Ménière's seemed to be pointing me toward that formless place where real instability was living in my life.

I found myself feeling touched and moved as I witnessed acts of kindness, offerings of welcome and inclusion, as well as musical lyrics chanting the praises of love. How liberating it was to feel and taste, allowing for analytic reviews to become pale. At the risk of fearing that I was succumbing to excessive sentiment, again, I wanted more.

Change was also taking place as I sat in the waiting room

of my physical therapist. In the past, I would feel an aversion to folks with twisted or missing limbs. I was compelled to confirm that I was something more, having no real clue what I possessed more of. Now, my breath was more rhythmic. My shoulders dropped and my jaw loosened. Had my days of unexpected immobilization opened me to my humanity and that of the folks in the waiting room? All the copious attention and affirmation I received for my physical appearance as a younger man had condemned me to an overflow of vanity. As it happens, an old definition of the word *vanity* is "empty." I had indeed settled for the emptiness of vanity and its obsession with looking good enough rather than the taste of genuine self-love. I began to believe that the unfortunate status of having Ménière's was morphing into an opportunity to decide how I wanted to age.

Ray and I continued to discuss how we wanted to grow into our aging. We both were acquainted with men and women whose aging we respected. Yet, it seemed we were being asked to bring our visions to who we wished to be in our elder years. I was reminded of the mythologist Michael Meade, who distinguishes "elders" from "olders." He writes: "The elders carry a greater vision of life because they develop insight into their own lives. They face up to whatever fate had in store for them and found threads of destiny amidst the illusions and delusions of life."

Had I developed enough insight into life, affording me greater vision? Had I found the threads of purpose and meaning amidst the illusions and delusions of life? Could being an elder be like being a teacher? A person could not be a teacher without students. So, how could I be an elder without someone wanting me to be an elder to them? And what might that look like? I decided it might mean being viewed as a valued resource. Teachers become agents of schools and colleges, or they offer seminars, training sessions, or workshops. I wondered what kind of medium supports eldering someone. Then, I found Emma.

It didn't take long for me to figure out that being an elder was mostly an offering to give to myself. Unlike being a teacher, apprenticing to elderhood seems to point away from something outside the self for validation. The elder needs to be ready to serve if there are those seeking to be served. However, elderhood does not appear to depend on those seeking guidance knocking on the elder's door. My days with Emma offered significant edification regarding the relationship I was being asked to have with myself. The bedrock of that relationship was unconditional self-love reflected in a lifelong commitment to remain a student of genuine humility.

Most of my conversations about aging with colleagues and friends revealed a disinterestedness in succumbing to the cultural invitation to "get out of the way." It appeared that aging folks had two choices: fade into oblivion or enjoy the view from a golf course followed by several rounds of martinis. I began to acknowledge and accept that I had simply never been here before. Then again, my whole life had been a series of stages where I had never been before. The only difference was that my culture offered some guideposts for those earlier stages—maybe not so much about how to be thirty or forty, but more in the way of aging being simply "okay." Being seventy-three did not appear to be acquiring a cultural blessing, and there were far too many golfers and connoisseurs of fine martinis holding rank in their seventies.

It became increasingly clear that I would need help to explore both what aging meant for me and what a soulful path to elderhood might look like—hence, Emma. The first question coming to mind for the reader will be, "Is Emma a real person?" The answer is yes, insofar as she serves as my psychotherapist and mentor. There are several ways in which Emma has inspired the creation of what you are about to read. While

Emma is sometimes quoted verbatim, I also paraphrase conversations between Emma and myself. Sometimes, I share faint memories of our exchanges, which have taken on lives of their own. Lastly, Emma is the muse for my animated and active imagination.

My wish for you as the reader is that you might discover your own Emma, either in an elder willing to offer you care and guidance as you step somewhere you've never been before, or as an inner source of inspiration. Of course, I would be delighted if you could taste the words and vision on the following pages, offering you an opening into more sweetness.

1: MEETING EMMA

"One of the most beautiful gifts in the world is encouragement. When someone encourages you, that person helps you over a threshold you might otherwise never have crossed on your own."

– John O'Donohue

How does an aging man honor his aging in a culture obsessed with an unbridled adoration of youth? We live in a death-denying, age-deploring culture. With these two denials permeating our lived experience, aging is reduced to something unfortunate. We spend our early adulthoods and mid-lives working hard. If we're lucky, the hard work reflects a vocation, a path that chooses us, asking for our strengths and gifts. If the way is not so fortuitous, we work hard to put food on the table, pay bills, and educate our children. Either way, our culture frowns upon the accumulation of years and the closing out of our work life. It encourages us to simply enjoy a martini, play golf, and not get in the way of real life.

Five years ago, I discovered how much the culture had penetrated my alleged inoculation against ageism. I decided to do some work on my relationship with my aging. I asked a friend whom he might recommend. He suggested a woman named Emma and pointed out that she was in her early eighties. I moved into an extended pause. She was at least thirteen years older than me.

"What are you thinking about?" my friend asked.

"Well, that's kind of old," I muttered, trying and failing to stop the words from leaving my lips, concerned about how my friend might see me.

"Right, that is kind of old, but I thought you wanted to work on aging," he added with a gaze suggesting that I might be taking on a task larger than I anticipated.

Well, my friend was right. I discovered that I had an adversarial relationship with aging. I had made it the enemy, and it was winning the battle. I went ahead and made an appointment to see Emma, as uncomfortable as I was. I began thinking back to my days as an altar boy in the Catholic church attended by my family. I had a particular memory of being thirteen years old and serving at a 7:00 AM weekday mass. Just before passing out communion, I turned to see who would be receiving it and noticed a congregation of seven older women. That was the last mass at which I ever served as an altar boy.

My adolescent ego could not bear participating in an event attended only by a small group of old women. What did that say about me? It seemed like something was being taken from me, but I had no clue what it was. Years later, I saw that I had some sexism woven through my ageism. Hanging out with a group of old ladies early in the morning did not speak admirably to my virility. The very notion of it was a threat to my self-image. At sixty-seven, could I possibly still be running out of that church?

I began to wonder whether eldering meant getting clear about a host of "isms" we likely all carry as a result of the indoctrination received from family, school, and church. Besides opening to my ageism and sexism, I reluctantly remained vigilant about the racism, ableism, and classicism that likely lurked just below the surface. I saw how easy it could be to occupy the high ground, accusing others of such depraved attitudes. In each case, I found fear to be the driving force. Eldering might be asking me to make peace with my fear, as well as take possession of all that I saw in the world and judged as sordid.

Lines from Thich Nhat Hanh's poem, "Please Call Me by My True Names," called me to this task:

I am the mayfly metamorphosing
on the surface of the river.
And I am the bird
that swoops down to swallow the mayfly.

I am the frog swimming happily
in the clear water of the pond.
And I am the grass-snake
that silently feeds itself on the frog.

I am the child in Uganda, all skin and bones,
my legs as thin as bamboo sticks.
And I am the arms merchant,
selling deadly weapons to Uganda.

I am the twelve-year-old girl,
refugee on a small boat,
who throws herself into the ocean
after being raped by a sea pirate.
And I am the pirate,
my heart not yet capable
of seeing and loving.

I am a member of the politburo,
with plenty of power in my hands.
And I am the man who has to pay
his "debt of blood" to my people
dying slowly in a forced-labor camp.

(Lines 13-36)

I decided that some form of healing might take place if I showed up in Emma's office. One week later, I arrived and was greeted by an eighty-one-year-old woman dressed in a flowing purple chiffon dress with a scarf of a lighter purple. She showed me into her small office, with one chair, a gray loveseat, a small bookcase, a vase with artificial purple flowers, and a Monet print hanging directly to the left of me as I sat on the loveseat.

"Paul, tell me what brings you here and how I might be of help," Emma said, her tone invitational, obviously comfortable in her role as a psychotherapist. Little did I know, my intentions to address aging in a few sessions led me to receive a measure of abiding mentorship.

"Well, I'm aging, and I'm not sure how accepting I am of it," I began, wanting to convey that I was here to be honest.

"I hear you saying that you're aging and that it's challenging you," she replied, not appearing to be at all concerned about my quandary.

"Yes, I don't feel like I'm at peace with my aging."

"It sounds like you think you are doing the aging," she responded.

"Well, it is me that I'm talking about," I added, somewhat puzzled by her remark.

"Quite the contrary. I don't think that you are doing the aging. Did you decide one day that you were going to do whatever you could to age?" she asked, leaving me intrigued.

"No, that never happened."

"Right, that never happened because you are not the one making aging happen. Life has been aging you. Did you ever consider that?" she inquired, leaving me to feel like I was embarking on Aging 101.

"I can't say that I have. Can you say more about life aging me?" I said, hoping that I was about to hear something I needed to hear.

"Sure, the truth is most folks protest aging because they know on some level that they are not in charge of it, that it's happening to them, regardless of their intentions or attitude about it. Life brought you a series of events and challenges to respond to and gave you a body that would degenerate in time. Life has been aging you," Emma reiterated, with an air of certainty that nevertheless lacked any note of condescension.

"Are you suggesting that aging is not really what is bugging me, but rather that life is in charge of it, that life is doing it to me?" I asked, starting to grasp Emma's thinking.

"Sure, it doesn't mean that you don't contribute to life aging you. The more you live in the tension of resisting how life ages you, the more you contribute to the aging process. The ego doesn't tolerate losing dominion over its experiences. In fact, most of us believe that we are the ones doing all the living. Well, the news is that life is mostly living us. Life has challenged you, called to you, shocked you, stimulated you, puzzled you, hurt you, thrilled you, and provoked you. All the while, you have convinced yourself of being the one living life. Of course, if you would have been honest all along about life living you rather than the illusion that you were mostly living it, then when life decided to age you, it would not be such a big deal," Emma explained with the matter-of-fact air of someone giving directions to the nearby convenience store.

"Wow, I guess I never looked at how much life was happening to me. I get that I had choices as life was happening, and I did decide that I was doing it all," I added, puzzled that I could have lived that long being confused all the while.

"Well, of course, the ego delights in deluding itself that it is the only show in town," explained Emma, her smile suggesting that the ego might only fool her so many times.

"I really want to address the nature of elderhood with you."

"That's a great topic. However, I think you need to take a

closer look at your relationship with aging. Who I
may discover something about aging as you do so.
ing about aging as a welcome to the soul."

"Soul, you say."

"Yes, soul. Does that sound strange?"

"No, I just didn't think of the soul and aging together," I
admitted.

"Oh, they go well together. Try writing about welcoming
the soul. You may find a soulful way to age, or possibly a soulful path to elderhood might begin to open up for you," she encouraged.

The idea of welcoming the soul really got my attention. We
spent the rest of that meeting talking about the men in my
family and the legacies they passed on. I decided to take
Emma's advice and explore welcoming the soul and more
about my relationship with aging by talking to folks and writing about it.

WELCOMING SOUL

May your stories grow, embellished by depictions of boldness,
grace, resolve, and forgiveness. Let these narratives find some
small place where the voices of the demons haunting your soul
continue to soften.

When the inevitable loneliness of the journey threatens to turn
you against yourself, remember those who came before you—
your ancestors, who prepared a place for you long before your
arrival.

May your betrothal to life be renewed by a single act of generosity and a quiet moment of gratitude, releasing the shackles
of victimization.

..et your heart exercise a fervent loyalty to the beliefs that en-
liven your spirit while holding your views with a suppleness
that allows you to greet a fresh idea like the possibility of a
new friend.

Do not look at your life gravely through the eyes of right and
wrong, but rather reach more deeply, beyond fear, to the place
where wonder, curiosity, and awe dwell.

When you look at the distance that separates who you are
from who you wish to be, remember that compassion offered
to who you are will inevitably be a welcome to who you wish
to be.

Remember how fitting it is that you remain engaged in a love
affair with the exploration of your inner world. May your life
possess enough peace and disturbance to keep you enthralled
with that love affair.

AGING

Emma's suggestion that I wasn't the one doing my aging continued to rattle around in my head. Questions began to surface: If I'm not aging myself, then is it possible that I'm not
living myself? What is aging? What happens to us when, as
Emma would put it, life ages us?

  I wanted to stay with this idea that life was living me. But
what did it mean? And if life had been living me, then what
had I been doing? At sixty-seven, I did figure out that I had
been pretending a great deal about how much of life was allegedly in my control. Thirty years ago, I was convinced that
at least seventy percent of my experience was in my control.
Now, I was willing to settle for five to seven percent.

The more honest I got about how much of life was out of my control, the more I could see the fear behind the pretense. I was scared to accept that life was essentially unpredictable, mysterious, and insecure. Life could take the breath out of my body during the night, eliminating the following day. I compensated for my fear of life's nature with the size of my will, my sense of what could be accomplished, and my decisions and choices. Illusions of grandiosity frequently brought me to an adversarial encounter with the people, places, and events that showed little or no interest in cooperating with my will. I even infused my protests with some alleged form of power. Caught in an adolescent holding pattern, I seemed to believe that my complaints would somehow influence the gods and get them to respond more favorably to my will.

Could it be that life was not simply trying to frustrate me? No, what life was doing was consistently revealing its immensity and unpredictable nature. I was too frightened to accept it. However, it gets difficult to mature emotionally with a significantly distorted view of life. I began to wonder how I could meaningfully live a life that was so beyond my control? Was living not so much about me? What would possibly be gained? Wouldn't life be mostly about defeat and powerlessness? If so, then aging would be about only defeat and powerlessness.

DEFEAT AND POWERLESSNESS

Aging is unacceptable when we do not yet know—or we forget—how to live. When a journey is mysterious, unpredictable, and insecure, it guarantees defeat and powerlessness. In the words of Ralph Ellison, "Life is to be lived, not controlled; and humanity is won by continuing to play in face of certain defeat." Guided by these words, we can ask: What does it mean to live life rather than control it? How is humanity won when we play in the face of certain defeat? First of all, the ego abhors the notion that controlling life is not what it's all about. The ego is quite reluctant to surrender its alleged dominion over life. Such reluctance sets the stage for a struggle characterized by an adversarial relationship with life.

Let's look at what commonly occurs when we attempt to dominate life. To be sure, feeling defeated by life is inevitable. Common responses to defeat include cynicism, resentment, and distrust. "You pay taxes, and then you die," as the adage goes. Life is confirmed to be the enemy, accompanied by a loss of faith and meaning. Anger easily becomes the principal motivating energy.

Another response to defeat can be to feel victimized by life. This response is characterized by a collapsing energy or depression. The tendency is to turn against yourself with a host of self-incriminating accusations, all aimed at suggesting you simply don't have what it takes to create a fulfilling life. The victim's posture easily leads to "I'm not going to play in the face of certain defeat." This response results in a crisis of faith and meaning.

Guiding the ego to come into a rightful relationship with an unpredictable journey can be an arduous psychological task. Thus, taking life seriously leads to a crisis of faith and meaning. It is important not to catastrophize or turn against ourselves when we are in someone—or something—else's grip.

Old meanings of the word *bless* include "to speak well of and wish well to." It seems fitting to bless the experience of this crisis and the person in the middle of such a predicament.

A BLESSING FOR A CRISIS OF FAITH

When you take your beliefs seriously,
they are neither borrowed nor held casually.
Your beliefs reflect a loyalty of heart.
They serve to guide decisions and choices.
Of course, there is the hidden expectation that life will
confirm the value and legitimacy of your beliefs.
Fate, however, may have a different plan.

This plan shows itself to be quite incongruent with your best belief.
You may find yourself facing loss due to the death of a loved one
or feeling betrayed by someone to whom you gave your loyalty.
Or you may be facing some catastrophic illness.
Some upset has challenged your trusted beliefs.

Now, you are lost as a crisis of faith descends upon you.
When you stand, no longer knowing what to believe,
you will feel like something in you is dying.
Something is also attempting to be born,
which may be more difficult to see.
Be gentle with your uncertainty
for it is the womb of some belief destined for your heart.

Allow the uncertainty to be a declaration of a
maturing spirit driven by curiosity and wonder, seeking its home.
Do not rush to clarity, which will likely yield some imposter,
a belief attempting to quell the accompanying quaking uncertainty.
The gestation of renewed faith needs time to let go of the old
while preparing for the new.

Life tends to both give a great deal and ask for a great deal.
Let your crisis of faith be a reminder that life
asks you to dream, believe, and become deeply disillusioned,
only to find the courage to dream and believe again.
Only then may you discover that no single belief
was ever destined to guide you home.

Let's look now at a blessing for a crisis of meaning:

A BLESSING FOR A CRISIS OF MEANING

The story you now live in constitutes the current meaning of your life.
These stories are organic.
They are meant to serve, then fade away,
giving rise to a new narrative.
We are asked to muddle about as one story ends
while the next has yet to begin.
This muddling can be seen as a crisis of meaning.
The muddling is psychic labor,
releasing one story while incubating the next.

Simplicity can hold you during your incubation.
Let go of your attachment to generating an impressive story.
Do not rush the gestation period.
Be mindful of who you are in the here and now.
You may be in a story of washing the dishes,
talking to a friend, organizing your closet, or taking a walk.
These are all simple stories to be in and are quite honorable.

There is simply no other way to grow up.
You are a meaning-maker, and you make meaning
as you understand what is in your interior landscape
that deserves your attention and devotion.
Come to trust your instincts, your values, and your longing.
In such trust, you belong to yourself.
Allow this belonging to deepen,
yielding your meaning as you are touched and moved.

Life will call you to unsolvable situations involving loss,
betrayal, suffering, defeat, and bewilderment.
You will need to decide who you are beyond knowing
what is right or fitting.
When integrity guides you,
your decisions come from that inner landscape.

When the darkness of muddling descends upon you,
you will always have, "I am the one seeking meaning."

In a crisis of meaning, as you are muddling,
remember those times of integrity.
However, sometimes, the muddling involves
a shift in values and what is desired.
Return again and again
to the simplicity of living in the here and now.
The present moment knows how to hold you as a meaning-maker.
Let go of ambitions and find meaning in settling into the moment.

RETURNING TO EMMA'S

"I'm wondering if you are ready to say goodbye to midlife," asked Emma with the lightness of one bidding farewell to friends after an enjoyable evening.

"Well, I haven't thought about it," I responded.

"Maybe you should. We can look at life separated into three distinct parts. The first third is about getting here and is driven by some important questions: What was given to me by my parents? What was taken from me by my parents? How free do I feel to claim how I might be different from the tribe I come from? What do I truly desire? How do I get ready to live that desire? The middle third is about achieving and accomplishing, guided by these questions: What are my gifts? How can I best manifest them? Who can I collaborate with? What do I want to achieve? How will I know when I've attained this achievement? The last third of life is about getting ready to leave with the following questions guiding the way: What have I given and what have I received from life? What is life now asking of me? What do I need to forgive about myself? What do I need to do or say to help me get ready to leave this life? What is my spiritual task?"

"I can see remnants of stage two in my life and a certain attraction to stage three. I'm not really sure what attracts me to stage three. Maybe it's the permission to look back as honestly as I can and know myself from this retrospective position," I added.

"What do you see when you look back?"

"Do you know Jean-Paul Sartre?"

"I do."

"He once noted, 'There is no traced out path to lead man to his salvation; he must constantly invent his own path. But, to invent it he is free, responsible, without excuse, and every hope lies with him.' I think that I am constantly inventing my own path, screwing up occasionally," I shared, noticing my eyes moisten and feeling touched anew by Sartre's words as I recalled both the joy and the struggle of such an invention.

"I believe you have, to the best of your ability," remarked Emma with a warm smile.

I let the silence sit with us after Emma's response, allowing her statement to wash over me like a tender, warm breeze.

"I want to hear your thoughts about aging," Emma invited with a tone that suggested she expected to hear something unique from me.

"I think that I'm starting to see that the big issue around aging is that it is so much more difficult to pretend that I have some control over it. I mean, the loss of strength I feel as a cyclist and even the damn mirror don't hesitate to remind me about aging," I added.

"Yes, for sure, aging should, at the very least, be a wake-up call concerning how much pretending about control you've been doing all of your life," reiterated Emma.

"I think that I'm more accepting about just how much defeat and powerlessness are part of the journey," I suggested.

"Do you know why defeat is such a prevalent theme in most people's lives?" she asked.

"I guess because so much is out of our control."

"Certainly, a great deal is out of our control. However, most defeat happens because we're so determined to control the uncontrollable," Emma declared, eyebrows arching upward.

"I've been thinking and writing about that and how much it brings us to a crisis of faith and a crisis of meaning. Does that make sense to you?" I asked, hoping for a measure of agreement.

"Absolutely! A crisis of faith is natural, since we are hopefully destined to outgrow many of our beliefs. Of course, when you carry distorted beliefs about how much control you allegedly have, you come to know an inordinate amount of defeat and the accompanying crisis of faith. And a crisis of meaning will occur with these distorted beliefs as you strive to be in some splendid story rather than accept living an ordinary life," Emma stressed, her voice taking on an instructive tone.

"I don't think I've ever heard anyone talk about themselves as living an ordinary life—at least, not with a note of acceptance and joy. I hear you promoting such an attitude. However, I must confess, I haven't ever found myself longing for an ordinary life," I pointed out with a hint of embarrassment, as if I had been doing it wrong.

"Of course, you haven't. I'm guessing you were never told that living in an ordinary story was something to pursue. Or, for that matter, you were never told what living in an ordinary story might look like," she explained, her jaw tightening, showing some irritation with a culture that had failed to give me clarity about living in an ordinary story.

"Well, I'm thinking I just assumed that living an ordinary life would mean I'm—"

"It would mean that you were ordinary and not special. And if you're not special, then what would make you lovable? It was a kind of distorted love story. Rather than offering acceptance for who you are, you were in pursuit of being better," she added before I could finish my sentence, and the sentiment was right on, leaving me aware of my striving to be special.

"I gotta admit, I don't really get what being ordinary and lovable have in common," I acknowledged, knowing that something important was escaping me.

"That's not unusual. However, being ordinary and lovable is extremely sustainable," Emma suggested, unable to hold back her convincing smile.

"I'm not sure what you mean by 'sustainable' in regard to being ordinary."

"Are you familiar with a protocol that the Roman Senate generated concerning the return of their victorious generals?"

"No, I'm not."

"Well, the Roman Senate feared that the generals might be on a victory binge and return home with aspirations of crowning themselves emperor. So, they made it a law that a returning general could ride into Rome only accompanied by his personal guards, leaving his army on the outskirts of the city. Also, a horseman was designated to ride alongside the returning general, whispering, 'Glory is but fleeting.'"

"I think I get what the sustainability of the ordinary might mean," I offered, thankful for the example.

"I recommend you create more of a relationship with the notion of the ordinary by talking about it, writing about it, contemplating it, dreaming about it, and simply experiencing it as much as possible," Emma encouraged, her eyes widening, suggesting she knew that she was asking me to take on a task arduous for my ego.

A BLESSING FOR THE SACRED ORDINARY

It is only too easy to look beyond the sacredness of the sacred ordinary.
This gaze is driven by proving eyes,
eyes determined to demonstrate how special you are.
Draped in the cape of special, you become
convinced that you are lovable.
However, a testimony of love is extremely mercurial,
elusive to sustainability.

Of course, to maintain special,
you must prove it again and again.
These varied accomplishments, one by one,
easily morph into an insatiable begging for some finer triumph,
something more robust than your last achievement.
You can feel the hunger for a performance
that will truly reveal your mastery.

The seduction of special is palpable.
You can feel it running through your veins,
pushed from one end of you to the other with rushes of adrenalin.
Come to know your fix of special, and like cotton candy,
you see that it cannot nourish.
It is a fleeting moment asking you to return to the sacred ordinary.

Your kinship with the ordinary places you in the
right relationship with yourself and with life.
Life is mostly a series of what appears common and customary.
However, within this commonness, there is an endless
opportunity for unique experiences,
asking you to find what has been waiting for you.

Welcome the four handmaidens of the sacred ordinary:
simplicity, authenticity, curiosity, and wonder.
Simplicity will help you peel away distractions.
Authenticity will allow you to get honest about
who you are in the moment.

Curiosity summons a level of care
for what lies in the unique moment.
Wonder provides faith in possibility.

As you hold the faith that this sacred ordinary moment
is where you belong,
you come to know your unique experience, your unique self.
Something to prove escapes you,
as does the attachment to being special.
Now, you have come home to yourself,
greeted by a welcome permeated with a sustained deservedness.

I began to look forward to my time with Emma, as I knew
how much of a resource she would be with respect to my
eldering. As I paid attention to the sacred ordinary, I became
increasingly curious about how to create a meaningful relationship with the here and now.

2: THE INITIATION

"At critical junctures, outer trouble and the inner need to grow con-
spire to set each of us on a path of awakening and initiation."

– Michael Meade

"I imagine you want to get back to talking about elderhood,"
offered Emma, ready to pursue the topic.

"Yes, of course! I know that I'm not interested in simply
getting older. I want my aging to have some meaning and purpose," I explained, excited to move forward.

"Then, we should talk about the Initiation," continued
Emma.

"Initiation! How do I get Initiated? Who does the Initiation?"

"Well, unfortunately, there won't be fellow elders gathering in their ritualistic garb and facilitating some elaborate cer-
emony. However, you can have a mentor and fellow travelers
for support," Emma offered, seemingly confident that this Initiation could happen.

"When will it begin?" I asked, hoping for something to
happen soon.

"Oh, it began long ago when you were inventing your own
path, which we have addressed. Each time you invented your
own path by separating from the prevailing ideology of the
culture, you stepped into an Initiatory process. Separation is

the first stage of an Initiation. We can say that you've been preparing for your elderhood all along," offered Emma, leaving me feeling quite confident and wondering if I might be offering myself too much credit.

"You mean I'm already there!"

"No, not quite. I'm simply saying that you laid some important early groundwork," she added, bursting into laughter.

"What do I need to do now?" I deferred, trying to hide my disappointment.

"I would recommend starting by appreciating how much opportunity life has already offered you for Initiation," Emma suggested, pointing me toward a new understanding of life.

"Well, there certainly were no carefully designed rituals guiding my Initiation," I added, implying that the elders had failed me.

"Sure, there were no rituals because we live in a ritual-barren culture. Life is about change, and change is about loss and separation. Loss is the Grand Initiator, and all Initiations begin with some form of separation. It can be a separation from a person, place, institution, or even an emotional disposition or a body part," she explained with an obvious investment in my understanding and our work together.

"Why is separation a herald of an unfolding Initiation?" I asked.

"Well, to 'initiate' literally means to begin something, and all beginnings are preceded by something ending or that which we're separating from," Emma pointed out matter-of-factly.

"What is supposed to happen after the separation?" I inquired.

"The hope is that a great deal will happen. Sometimes, the person being Initiated is excited and highly focused on whatever the separation is creating space for. It may be some form of achievement, an adventure, a relationship, or a new place to live or work. Other times, there may be grief with regard to what is ending. Both are natural responses, and sometimes, they are simultaneous. And then comes a host of Trials and Ordeals not obviously connected to what the Initiate was planning on. These challenges are meant to deepen and strengthen the Initiate's capacity to live life on life's terms. This might entail letting go of some measure of innocence and naïveté, especially concerning how much the Initiate believed he or she could control what happens. It also means that the Initiate gets more honest about fears and demons that dwell within. It is a time to learn to ask for help, letting go of compulsive self-reliance. Quite often, there will be a teacher or mentor who is available to offer guidance and encouragement. Of course, the Initiate will need to likely access a new level of humility to receive the assistance. Typically, Initiates gain more clarity about who they are and what life is asking of them beyond their initial quest," Emma detailed, leaving me feeling somewhat overwhelmed and convinced I was in the presence of someone who knew what she was talking about.

"Wow, it sounds like a great deal can happen during this stage," I said, concerned that I might not do well with these Trials and Ordeals.

"Yes, it depends on the courage and commitment of the Initiate concerning how much is learned and how much help is received to support the learning. This is a time of genuinely inventing the path that will be traveled by the Initiate," she explained supportively.

"Do the Trials and Ordeals mark the end of an Initiation?" I asked, hoping that what I heard was enough.

"No, there is a third stage, often called the Return. The hope is that you return to yourself, living more honestly about who you actually are. You also return to your people, family, friends, colleagues, and clients with a greater capacity to serve, affording you a genuine experience of belonging,"

Emma added, leaning forward, her tone gaining a crispness when she spoke of serving.

"I'm not sure where I am in my elderhood Initiation," I offered, hoping Emma might suggest that I was close to the end.

"You know, there's a lot to separate from as you age. Allow yourself to take inventory of what you are separating from within you as well as around you and the losses that ensue," Emma suggested with no hint of being attached to something happening at an accelerated pace.

I left Emma's that day feeling like an Initiation into elderhood could offer a more real possibility of bringing depth and meaning to aging and wondering whether I was up to the task.

SEPARATION

I often have the thought that most of my life is behind me. Most of my life has been lived with too many separations to count. Maybe I'm supposed to understand the idea of most of my life being behind me, at least in terms of the number, as opposed to the quality, of the years I have left. I explained this view to my fifty-year-old son recently. I've noticed that we meet more regularly since that conversation.

I can see that there may be multiple separations currently ushering me into an Initiation. I've been separating from the illusion that I'll be here forever, which includes a separation from the belief that tomorrow is guaranteed to me. I miss the comfort of living in the illusion of my life not ending. Emma was right about the loss being offered by a separation also presenting a gift. The gift appears to be a new kinship with the here and now.

Take Peter, for example, a retired architect who came in for his initial session with me, wanting to focus on the challenges of aging.

"Life is different now in my early seventies," he began with a look that suggested he hoped to be understood.

"What differences get your attention?" I asked, wondering, now that I was looking at aging through the lens of Initiation, whether Peter was facing some separation.

"Well, I'll tell you, I don't like the questions I'm asking about friends and acquaintances. I used to ask if so and so still lived at the same address. Now, I ask the same question followed by, 'Is he still alive?' I don't like this last question," concluded Peter.

"Yes, I understand that not to be a welcome question. And I'm wondering, besides the obvious, is there anything that the question symbolizes or implies for you?"

"It does remind me that most of my life is behind me and that death is closer than it once was," Peter revealed, his voice trailing off, and I was glad that we were of the same generation.

"I'm wondering whether death is closer now than it was thirty years ago or whether it might be that your acknowledgment of your mortality is more present with a lessening of your denial of death," I noted in the hope that my remarks would not be too off-putting.

"Yes, I think that's right. I certainly could have died thirty years ago. It's just that I carried more denial of my death then. I guess denial is a funny thing," Peter speculated.

I went on to explain to Peter that he could view his aging through the lens of an Initiation. From that perspective, we could say that he was separating from the level of denial he previously carried about dying. He appeared to be quite open to learning more about seeing his aging as an Initiation. Upon arriving at our next session, he wanted to inventory several separations he was experiencing.

"You know, I can't remember names for the life of me—

authors, actors, singers, and acquaintances. They're all fading away into the ether," he declared, not appearing to feel burdened by the loss.

"You seem okay with not being able to exercise the recall you had twenty years ago," I reflected.

"The more we talk about aging as an Initiation, the more I'm willing to stop fighting it. I mean, there are all kinds of changes or separations I could fight with," he shared with a note of resignation even as I heard my own dynamic of protest against aging.

"Tell me more about what's going on with you," I encouraged.

"Sure. I'm separating from a level of vitality, calling me to afternoon naps. I pee more during the night, separating me from an uninterrupted night's sleep. I'm separating from the confidence that I can easily back out of a grocery store parking lot. I can't imagine how I ever was able to look in so many directions while backing up! I'm separating from being able to enter the world freely without proper visual and audio aids— you know, my glasses and my hearing aids. Have you ever tried wearing glasses, hearing aids, and a pandemic mask? When I look in the mirror, I'm separating from a younger man who had beautiful, thick, curly hair. I miss him. After hearing about friends falling while walking on snow or ice, I'm separating from the confidence to take a stroll in those kinds of conditions. Just between you and me, I'm separating from being able to be sexual more than once per day," Peter conceded with sustained eye contact, suggesting he might be feeling okay about revealing this much yet concerned about my reactions.

Listening to Peter offered me more insight into how separations can point to the possible upcoming Trials and Ordeals.

TRIALS AND ORDEALS

The ordeal of aging, writes James Hollis in *The Middle Passage: From Misery to Meaning in Midlife*, is "most commonly of further separation so that the initiate might learn there is a strength within to meet the task without." Thus, my work with Peter prepared me to return to Emma's, eager to think through together what his next step in an elder Initiation might look like.

"I'm understanding how the Separation is significantly about something ending," I suggested.

"That's right. What do you notice ending for the architect you are working with?" asked Emma.

"He's more than willing to identify the losses he experiences due to aging. Can we talk more about how the losses relate to the second stage of the Initiation?"

"Sure. What to be clear about, first of all, is that your client won't go anywhere you haven't been. If you don't accept aging, he won't either," reassured Emma.

"Why is that?"

"It's a lot like not being willing to hire a guide who has never been beyond 5,000 feet on a mountain to take us up to 20,000 feet," she explained.

"Yeah, I get that, but how does the client know where we've been or not been?" I wondered.

"I'm not sure anyone knows how clients know, but they do. The irony is that they will often choose a practitioner who hasn't gone so they can take refuge in their resistance and not go themselves," Emma explained. I had never imagined such a motivation to not work with a therapist.

"The good news is that I am willing to let go of my protest against aging. I'm not sure whether the fullness of acceptance is in yet, and I'm willing to continue to work on it," I promised myself as well as Emma, wondering what it would take to interrupt my protesting.

"The first stage of Separation guarantees loss. It's necessary to grieve the loss of the familiar, and that's a big loss in aging. The key is to grieve the losses without getting stuck in feeling angry about what has fallen away. Is your client still feeling angry?" Emma asked.

"Yes, he is still angry. And I am reminded that such anger is mostly the ego's way of avoiding feeling helpless about not being able to stop the aging from happening. I do see that I need to allow myself to feel shamelessly helpless in my own Initiation," I added.

"Feeling the helplessness is key to unfolding some real acceptance of the aging process," Emma agreed, her tone gaining a level of gravitas.

"I gotta admit, I feel like a real novice when it comes to genuine acceptance of the losses issued by aging," I offered.

"Certainly, the ego wants its youthful prowess maintained as well as the delusion that it will live forever. The ego delights in its alleged mastery over life, taking sanctuary in a deluded story of power. Aging simply reminds us about who is really in charge. The ancient definition of the word *fate* is 'will of the gods.' It certainly makes a statement about who's really in charge, doesn't it?" Emma explained, laughing heartily.

"From that perspective, it sounds like aging is simply clarifying what was always true: namely, that fate or people, places, and events define most of our lives. I can see that we create who we are by how we respond to fate, rather than having some aggrandized view of how much we controlled or intended," I added.

"Yes, and in aging, because of what is taken away, we have a large opportunity to get right with life. Stop playing games about who is in charge. We can say that the real purpose of Trials and Ordeals is to give Initiates the chance to get right with themselves, becoming more honest about who they are and more accepting of life's immensity. It certainly is no wonder that an old definition of the word *trial* is 'the way the genuineness or correctness of something may be determined,'" Emma assured, reminding me of how much work authentic elderhood called for.

"It sounds like if we have significantly drifted away from ourselves in our youth, a trial could feel quite demanding and even daunting," I offered.

"Absolutely. It's like traveling a long way from home. The return trip is going to be somewhat wearisome. The key is to remain close to what the trial is asking for and to neither shame the request nor who you have been. Remain mindful that the trial is simply offering you an opportunity to get right with yourself without hurting you in some way. My guess is that your client Peter is getting closer to a more intense trial since he has accepted the Initiatory process of his aging," Emma explained, leaving me to feel like the work Peter and I were doing was moving in the right direction.

Several weeks later, Peter came in for a session and began to describe an ordeal he found himself in. It did not take me long to see what he was facing.

"I'm having a hard time with this younger architect named Jonah. He's only forty-two and certainly not as experienced as I am. The president of our organization thinks he's the Second Coming. Whenever she gets a request for a speaker, Jonah gets the nod. He's a kind of architectural guru. However, he's a flâneur and probably doesn't know the difference between a contemporary structure and a modernist one. He's likely not able to creatively address the prevailing hegemony. He's not able to determine where a building's gesture should be placed," barked Peter, his annoyance eclipsing his inflated posture.

"Wow! You've got a lot going on regarding this Jonah fellow. What's a 'flâneur,' and what do you mean by 'gesture'?" I asked.

"Oh, it's just architectural jargon," he responded, settling down a bit as he sat back in his chair, apparently gathering himself.

"What's really going on with you and this guy? I'm wondering if you feel the need to compete with him," I suggested, the energy of his competitive spirit bouncing off the office walls.

"It does sound that way, doesn't it?" he admitted.

"Tell me, how might being competitive with him serve you?"

"It's just that he's getting a great deal of attention," Peter emphasized.

"Okay, so what happens to you when Jonah gets attention?"

"I—I—I'm not sure. Obviously, something happens that ain't feeling so good," Peter responded, dropping his head as if the weight of it were succumbing to the force of gravity.

"Peter, close your eyes and just breathe into where the not-so-good feeling is in your body and take your time," I invited.

"I think I feel jealous. Why should he get so much positive attention?" he suggested with less assertion.

"It's not always easy to be honest about feeling jealous. I like to remind myself that jealousy is about some alleged loss. Do you experience some loss as Jonah gets the attention?" I wondered, hoping he could welcome whatever loss waited for his attention.

"Well, he's the dude!" Peter boomed, his eyes tearing up in a way that made it hard to tell whether he was crying or laughing. "Yes, Jonah is the dude. And you ask what my loss is. Well, I'm not the dude," Peter continued, laughing with less exuberance yet conveying the silliness of dude-hood.

"Peter, your laughter suggests to me that you're having some important awareness about Jonah being the 'dude,'" I suggested.

"Oh yes, I am. I forgot about the seduction of being the dude. I give others the power to confirm my worth with their attention and their admiration. I can believe that my essential value isn't my responsibility. I don't really lose anything when Jonah is the dude in our organization. In fact, I have the chance to get right with my own goodness," he confirmed, reflecting a valued and in-depth understanding of this business.

"I want you to know that I respect what you're doing here. Seeing Jonah as the dude has become a significant Trial in your Initiation. You're right; you are allowing yourself to feel and know how tempting it is to give responsibility to others for confirming how important you are. That's a great thing to know. It allows you to come back to yourself and the willingness to hold your essential goodness since no one else can do it for you," I concluded, wanting Peter to feel the genuineness of my affirmation of his efforts.

"Thanks. I guess that this is what it means to move a bit closer to elderhood. It's like I'm releasing some attachment to others witnessing me. It feels quite liberating," he said with a clear note of satisfaction.

"I think that it is about a move closer to your elderhood. I'm wondering, now that you can let go of Jonah as an opponent, is there any other way you might relate to him?" I asked.

"He did get a prestigious architectural award a few weeks ago. I think I'll forward a note of congratulations. For some reason, that idea feels like more than a simple act of kindness."

"I also believe that it is more than a simple act of kindness. I would suggest that it is the act of witnessing a younger man's gifts and accomplishments. It is the action of a genuine elder," I added, not holding back the fervor of my respect for Peter.

I was glad to report to Emma how Peter found his way through a powerful Trial. She immediately pointed out the value of my offering to him. I blushed and let her know that I was well versed in viewing another man as the dude and allowing competitive energies to either run consciously or un-consciously. She quickly noted how often she heard me delight in blessing a younger man. I quietly acknowledged how much my relationship with Emma was a place for me to strengthen my ability to receive, which was a strong expression of my Initiation.

THE RETURN

I was eager to discuss with Emma the nature of the Return, the final stage of an Initiation.

"It helped to see myself in Peter's Trial," I pointed out.

"Yes, that's critical. When you saw yourself in his Trial, you could then easily hold what the Trial was asking for. You were able to mentor him well," Emma affirmed, her smile conveying her appreciation of the work.

"Thanks. Can we look more closely at the Return? How does it begin and what happens?" I asked.

"I don't think anyone really knows how the Return begins. It is as if the soul has what it came for. Life may offer opportunities for rest and renewal as Trials and Ordeals fade into the background. In an elderhood Initiation, there is a return to something older, maybe even ancient, that was always part of the soul but blurred by excessing ego aspirations or a need for more healing. We can say that there is a return to something interior and something exterior, and hopefully sustainable," Emma explained, her chin lifting slightly in a subtle expression of confidence.

"How would you describe what can be returned to in the interior world?" I asked.

"Lessons learned set the stage for what can be returned to in the interior landscape. For example, your architect client laughed at his competitive energy aroused by the younger man whom he viewed as the 'dude.' That laughter was likely the start of a return to some expression of authentic humility. He was creating space for another man to receive a worldly acknowledgment, which is both an honoring of his own limits and quite generous. He was returning to a capacity he always had for humility and generosity, and with those traits in place, your client will serve the community," Emma noted with a sense of satisfaction in her voice, leading me to believe that she was getting as much as I was from our meetings.

"It seems to me that the idea of service is particularly important for the elder. I came across the following from Francis Weller," I offered. "'Initiation is meaningless outside the village. We need something to serve: We do this for the sake thereof. In other words, initiation was not meant for the sake of the individual; it was done for the welfare of the greater circle to which they belong. Initiates returned to the village, the community, or tribe, as newly created members of the wider cosmos. They were now authorized to participate in the care and maintenance of the community.'"

"Weller appears to understand the value of service. The capacity to serve happens when the Initiate can hold what is truly sustainable in life. We could say that devotion to what is sustainable makes the elder a bearer of light. Some questions support a continued inquiry aimed at identifying what is truly sustainable. I suggest you give the business of the Return some consideration along with what kinds of questions ultimately support sustainability," she offered, appearing confident that I would joyously take on the task.

TWELVE QUESTIONS TO LIVE WITH

I found myself preoccupied with the idea of what is truly sustainable. More than ever, it appears to be critical for elders to find clarity about what it means to create a sustainable relationship with life and to be bearers of light. We advocate being educated. Acquiring wealth, fame, and popularity are regularly endorsed as ways to approach life. Elders need to move beyond whether or not life is allowing for some agency of ego. This new approach to life entails getting honest about what it might take to create a meaningful and sustainable relationship with it. It may be a bit challenging to accept life as being essentially about change and uncertainty. However, if we can accept that, we can then explore what it takes to have a relationship with such a journey.

Below are some questions that may sustain an elder's focus on the path. The invitation is to live with rather than by these questions. Where the latter suggests that each question gets a neat and tidy answer and all is well, the former reflects a commitment to respond to them throughout our lives, allowing them to refresh and renew our relationship with ourselves while deepening our capacity to be fully alive. To live with these questions, a refinement of pride must happen. Rather than be guided by undaunted certainty, we can engender an abiding curiosity that shepherds our beliefs and choices. These questions will also call forward other questions meant to deepen our connection to ourselves and our experiences.

THE TWELVE QUESTIONS

1) **Where Do I Come From?** This is a foundational question related to family and cultural legacies. We can think of legacies as the beliefs and attitudes we inherit from our ancestors. Clarifying this question may involve asking: Do I come from a pattern of domination or submission? What scripts define gender? Is there a history of alcohol abuse or dependency on mind-altering chemicals? How did family members define the meanings of their lives?

2) **What Are My Natural Gifts or Strengths?** This is a critical question that can help us avoid pursuits in which we don't belong. Our gifts are best expressed where others will benefit and where we are contributing to the general good. This question also points toward an acknowledgment and celebration of our uniqueness and likely points in the direction of our life's purpose. Often, just being curious about what we love yields clarity about our gifts.

3) **How Am I Wounded?** This question aims at revealing what we either received too much of (abuse) or too little of (neglect). Our maturation greatly depends on being honest about what we receive and letting go of idyllic notions of receiving just the right amount of everything. We employ defenses to protect us from feeling the grief and vulnerability that comes with our wounding. However, these defenses tend to overprotect, obstructing our capacities to give and receive love while handcuffing the expression of our talents. It can be helpful to ask: What defenses are limiting me? How do I deconstruct my defenses? What are my wounds asking for?

4) **What or Whom Do I Need to Let Go Of?** This question can point to where our time and energy need to be focused. It also supports staying in touch with life's impermanence. The hope is we can more easily make peace with change.

5) **What Do I Love?** This question helps us identify what is to be prioritized and protected. It can also help identify our gifts and, possibly, our life's purpose. Responses to this question may refine how we can best serve.

6) **What Is Life Currently Asking of Me?** This is one of my favorite questions. It is meant to be the complement to the question: What do I desire? When these two questions live in concert, our rapport with life is deepened. There is a diminishment of excessive self-orientation with a

willingness to be informed by our lived experience. The result can be a creative resonance with life.

7) **Who Is Coming with Me?** This is a wonderful question reflecting the depth of rapport in our lives. It is often accompanied by several other relevant questions: Who knows me? Who loves me? Whom do I love? With whom can true collaboration and co-creation occur?

8) **What Do I Fear?** This question often points to where courage needs to live, inviting us to consider some form of risk. Being clear about our fear can inform us about the options of either expanding to take a risk or contracting in favor of protection.

9) **What Is My Task?** This question can also shed some light on our purpose. There may be a particular task, such as asking for something we want or creating or building something. Our task may be to learn how to live in a larger story with a greater capacity for compassion, creativity, courage, and resiliency. From a spiritual perspective, we can ask: What did I promise the gods? Such a promise would be imbued with our purpose and give meaning to our death, for it would inevitably be about service.

10) **What Do I Need to Forgive About Myself?** When we do not take on the responsibility of forgiving ourselves, we live in a condemned past. When we forgive ourselves, we give away past transgressions and return our attention to the here and now. As Buddhist teacher Jack Kornfield reminds us, "We forgive ourselves when we give up all hope of having a better past." We enter the present with more compassion and freedom, liberating ourselves from being taken hostage by our mistakes.

11) **With Whom Do I Have Unfinished Business?** Our relationships are inevitably for the sake of refinement.

Sometimes, it is a story we carry about others not liking or appreciating us. It could entail anger or resentment we are carrying. Another option might be a need for us to offer an apology or some form of restitution for having hurt someone. Attending to our relationships can restore stability and serenity to our lives.

12) **How Do I Prepare for My Transition?** This is a death-and-dying question. Is my estate in order? Do I continue to practice closure in my relationships and with life events? Is there anything or anyone from my past asking for my attention? What does a "good death" mean for me?

Living with these questions means relinquishing an urgency to deliver an answer, where an answer is likely a way to ease the tension we feel when facing the unknown. An ancient definition of the word *answer* is "to respond to, as in a letter." This meaning suggests we remain in correspondence with life, allowing it to touch us and bring us closer to ourselves. As we understand more about who we are and what life reveals about itself, we live more in the embrace of biophilia, the love of life.

COURAGE AND COMPASSION

Emma and I spent time reviewing the twelve questions. Toward the end of the discussion, she asked what qualities must an elder have to live the questions. After some thought, I responded, "Courage and compassion."

COURAGE

The word *courage* appears to have its origin in both French and Latin, referring to "heart." I find myself preferring to view courage as a verb rather than a noun. We could say that courageous living is heartful or heart-swelling living. I can't say that I ever defined any of my thoughts as courageous or that I was engaged in courageous thinking. It seems that some action is necessary, even if it is as simple as writing the thought down. However, there is interior action when we choose to look honestly at ourselves. I don't consider looking a courageous act. We can look and respond by denying, shaming, ridiculing, and belittling what we see. What takes courage or heart is the welcoming of what we witness about ourselves.

Although I often hear courage referred to as fearless action, I can't imagine such a thing. Why would anyone need courage in the absence of fear? Any action unaccompanied by fear is likely somewhat mundane and practical, with little or no risk involved. We can say that courageous action involves fear, risk, and feeling vulnerable and driven by something heartful.

How does a vulnerable, frightening, risk-oriented action become heartful? The heart brings us to action when what lives at its depths yearns to be revealed. Expressions thereof include devotion, faith, love, compassion, loyalty, and longing.

As we are willing to live courageously, we eventually make peace with life as mysterious, insecure, and unpredictable. Courage is transformed into acceptance. Feeling vulnerable and frightened are not experienced as something to overcome but simply what it means to live the journey honestly.

If elders are willing to release their youth rather than carry the weight of losses accrued over time, less courage is needed to age with some measure of grace. The need for courage also morphs into serenity as years of living a self-examined life declare the essential nature of the human condition rather than the narcissistic account of an individual personality.

A BLESSING FOR COURAGE

A life well lived asks for a great deal from you.
Its bidding includes honesty, kindness, desire, and integrity.
However, these things find no place without courage.
Your life can easily be reduced to a caricature of
what it means to be up to living a life you can call your own.

Courage is so much larger than some infrequent act of heroism.
Each day calls for courage.
It calls for the ego to let go of its blueprint for how life is to be lived.
That very act is deeply courageous.
What's left is living life on life's terms,
which includes people, places, and events with their agendas.

Courage is relaxing into what life is asking of you.
Life won't surrender its mystery, unpredictability, and insecurity.
You can soften life's demands.
You'll need to engender a spaciousness and a suppleness,
allowing you to see how some demand might bring you
a strength that was always waiting for you.

Stretching the borders of what can be viewed
and accepted is courageous.
Unfortunately, there is not much choice.
You either live courageously or you don't.
Cowardice will inevitably descend upon you,
meaning you will settle to see yourself as a victim of life.
Your voice cries out,
"Life, you owe me, and you have done me wrong."

When you refuse to see what life might be offering you,
hidden in its demands, you step away from yourself.
Take many steps away from yourself, and your spirit withers,
allowing the prevailing winds to toss you about.
You will not know who you are or where you belong.
Apathy and cynicism eclipse living courageously.

Do not shame your fear of love.
Love promises joy, comfort, and fulfillment.
However, love only guarantees loss.
Someone will either walk away or someone will die.
Let love call you somewhere you've never been.
Be scared and courageously allow yourself
to be held in the crucible of love.

There may be no act more courageous
than welcoming what you find within.
In such a welcome is where love lives.
Such a welcome goes wherever you go.
It will be sensed and felt in your tone, gaze, and movements.
Such a welcome is an ambassador of love.

COMPASSION

Compassion is the vital living force of the soulful elder. We remain in an intimate relationship with life when we see a need and feel called to unite with ourselves and others compassionately. An old understanding of the word *compassion* is "to be able to step into the suffering of others," to be with the suffering of those around us. This is not an easy task as we can easily avoid the suffering of another when we are trying to deny our own suffering.

Elders accept the responsibility of making peace with their suffering. In this way, they can experience how much suffering unites us and how much each of us deserves to be acknowledged, welcomed, and comforted in our suffering. The compassionate voice says, "I suffer with you." We find our way to the depths of our humanity as we accept suffering as a significant link to others, traversing our biases, self-righteousness, and condescension. Suffering offers a place where we do not have to be alone or allow another to be alone. Divisiveness and isolation lose their clout when our hearts open with compassion as we allow suffering to be a place where we receive others because they suffer.

A BLESSING FOR COMPASSION

It is spoken about regularly in a variety of spiritual settings:
How do we come to know we are in the presence of compassion?
How do we know we are the recipient?
or when compassion flows from our hearts?
Compassion becomes known when what separates loses its dominion.

Much falls away when compassion enters the room.
What supports disconnection suddenly weakens.
Pretense withers, unable to hold itself up.
Scaffoldings supporting hierarchy crumble.
Attempts to impress leave like unwelcome intruders.
Compassion easily claims its power to unite.

It is as if unity gains a prestigious presence.
There is an unbridled attunement accompanied by a palpable resonance.
The one who suffers and the one who offers witness
come to know each other as pilgrims on a perilous journey.
Distortions about the nature of life
give way to a clear understanding of what it means to suffer.

Suffering is then understood as deeply human.
The charade casting pleasure and excitement
at the core of the human condition recedes,
now offering only some faint contribution to the journey.
We come to accept suffering
and the vulnerability, fear, and helplessness
that bring us to the deeper regions of who we are.

Compassion can also unite us to ourselves.
It can bring us into self-attunement as we interrupt shame

for having made a mistake.
It can take the place of ridicule for some defeat
and remove self-contempt for unrequited love.
Compassion can be an ongoing invitation
to bring peace to our inner worlds.

We live in a time when we need elders to be radically honest about the nature of life and what it means to commit to a sustained relationship with our lived experience.

Just when I thought that I had a handle on elderhood, Emma encouraged living more deeply and more lightly. It sounded like a contradiction to me. How do I go about living with more depth yet lightly? Emma's response was, "Stop trying to get life right and let life get you right." I began to realize how much effort and strain I exercised toward getting life right. The task of attempting to get life right was exhausting. My ego was determined to be in charge by making life adhere to my expectations, desires, and dreams. Occasionally, life saw fit to grant me some measure of cooperation. I told Emma that something was missing in my life, that my greatest efforts did not appear to be delivering all the supposedly promised fulfillment. After all, I was doing my best to get life right.

If Emma was on to something that could potentially benefit me, I knew I would need to become clear about how I could best let go of my attempts to get life right. After that, I would need to learn how to allow life to get me right. The more I thought about it, the more I saw this challenge as the cornerstone of a soulful path to elderhood.

3: BEFRIENDING THE HERE AND NOW

"Beware the barrenness of a busy life."

– Socrates

"I'm starting to see why acceptance of what is fading away as I age doesn't come easily. The ego has always had another deluded plan. I'm also seeing that when acceptance of aging is compromised, the tendency is to get lost in memory, in the idealization of the past," I concluded.

"Yes. And being lost in the past places us in a precarious relationship with the here and now—the place where life can be truly lived. That's not to say there's no place for holding on to endearing memories. The soulful path of the elder does not allow the here and now to lose credibility due to the allure of the past," she explained, leaving me curious about how to hold the sweetness of the past without taking up residency there.

"How can I get honest about my relationship with the moment?" I asked, knowing I was stepping onto new ground.

"Let the moment talk to you, telling you how it feels about the relationship it has with you. Do some active imagination, which offers a much more poignant account of your experience, not succumbing to an opaque reflection burdened by a logical and sanitized account of what is truly messy," encouraged Emma, with me appreciating how she regularly pointed me toward my imagination.

I could see how challenging it had been, and remained so, for me to be in the present and, in a strange way, how I had betrayed the moment and myself. I was determined not to turn against myself regarding this ordeal, but rather see it as part of the trials of my Initiation. I decided to reflect more, talk more, and write more about my relationship with the here and now. I decided it would be helpful to see my return to the moment happening in stages.

The idea that it may be worthwhile to live as much as possible in the here and now seems to have been reduced to a minor spiritual axiom. Recently, while having dinner with an old friend who has enjoyed a generous amount of professional success, I heard a reference to the here and now as an extraneous cliché: "I know I should pay more attention to living in the present, but the excitement of my books booming and my artwork gaining newfound notoriety just pulls me into a 'what's next' orientation toward living." I heard myself in my friend's declaration and was curious about how each of us had developed such a cavalier attitude toward living where we belong, in the here and now.

I began to wonder how it is that folks who care about how they live take on such a casual attitude toward living in the here and now. I witnessed them pulled back to the present by the loss of a loved one, suffering from a catastrophic illness, or as the result of surviving a serious accident. Is that what it takes to return to the moment? I felt some resistance regarding having to wait for one of those kinds of events to move me into the present.

I decided it was likely that I and others did not live in the here and now simply because it was fun to jump to the next moment. There had to be something about the present that offered more than the joy and delight of living. My hope was that understanding what actually can take place in the here and now might offer some clarity about how to reenter it mindfully. What began to unfold was the possibility of five stages, not necessarily happening sequentially, that might give some guidance.

Emma and I spent a good deal of time talking about the importance of the here and now and what made it so difficult to live there. I began to realize that a genuine expression of elderhood greatly depended on being able to release my attachment to the future. I saw my propensity to sanitize reality by creating some idyllic version of possibility, some wonderful future happening. It was becoming clearer that, before my elderhood would be at hand, I would need to be willing to live life on life's terms.

STAGE ONE:
An Unconscious Adversarial Relationship

Contrary to how much applauding is done about a life lived in the here and now, by both spiritual and philosophical traditions, more may need to be said about such a choice. Children instinctively figure out on a preconscious level that the present is a lovely place to live as well as the only place where hurt, exclusion, and shame take place. Thus, the present has a double-edged identity, one allowing for love, creativity, and generativity and the other for pain and rejection. The psyche is better equipped to support a need to be protected from what may be injurious than what brings about fulfillment. Children decide to leave the here and now instinctively and unconsciously in favor of relocating to the alleged safety of the future.

Taking up residency in the future is anything but a cavalier shift. It is a desperate move to secure protection from the inevitable perils befalling the present. The here and now has unconsciously become the enemy, and we scramble feverishly toward the alleged sanctuary of the next moment and the next, until we accumulate months and years that have not been lived.

STAGE TWO:
A Conscious Adversarial Relationship

Stage one does not allow for much movement since it is lived unconsciously. Stage two means getting honest about the alleged glamor and charm alluring you to the future. However, I must at least be willing to acknowledge the inherent challenges waiting for me in the here and now. A conscious adversarial relationship with the here and now suggests I may not be ready to create an armistice with the present. Either way, it does mean I am aware of how and why an adversarial relationship was created. I become more cognizant of who may be waiting for me in the present: someone who is lonely, frightened, lost, or brokenhearted.

I could continue to decide that the here and now is the enemy. In which case, the parts of myself waiting there for me will feel disfavored and exiled. These displaced parts of the self tend to operate like real people who have been banished. They bang on the door of the psyche, seeking inclusion and leaving us feeling the angst and inner quaking of their protest.

As long as the moment and who is waiting for me there are seen as enemies, I will need to fortify my psychological garrison. These defenses may include alcohol, drugs, sugar, or simply a consistent state of frenzy, leaving me spinning from moment to moment as both my actions and speech speed away from the present.

It is common to hear great exhortations regarding the excitement for those living in stages one and two. "Did that excite you?" "What do you have planned that is exciting for the holiday?" "Did planning your trip get you excited?" The urgings toward feeling excited as much as you can seem endless. The energy of excitement is located in the throat and face. It appears that we are constantly encouraged to avoid the lower emotions such as sorrow, sadness, hurt, and grief, all of which drive us away from grounding ourselves in the here and now.

STAGE THREE:
A Conscious Non-Adversarial Relationship

This stage is marked by acceptance of how it served me as a child to relocate to the future. It also involves accepting that I am asked to live life on life's terms, which means accepting both the delight and the ordeals waiting for me in the moment. Most of all, it means opening my heart to all the parts of me waiting to be welcomed by living in the moment.

I don't recommend attempting to create a conscious, non-adversarial relationship with the here and now by yourself. Shifting your attitude toward the present from as a foe to as a friend can be an arduous psychological task. You will be undoing levels of denial as well as deepening the quality of your acceptance. This calls for robust emotional resiliency and new levels of heart opening. Let yourself be accompanied by someone acquainted with the territory, such as a mentor, who can help ease the transition into being more awake and more at home with yourself.

STAGE FOUR:
A Relationship Founded on Gratitude

As you become more familiar with yourself as the person who has decided to make peace with the here and now, you will be touched by the bounty of life's offerings. The present offers a large opportunity to encounter beauty, kindness, and inspiration. Nothing avails us more of the depth and breadth of life than being able to say, "I am here now."

A good friend has experienced a severe illness that has escorted him to the here and now. He returns from his medical appointments expressing gratitude for the kindness that the staff shows him. "The nurses, technicians, and doctors greet me, inform me, and guide me with clarity and respect from one test to another. I even get a call, several hours after returning home, from a nurse wanting to know how I'm doing." When I hear these kinds of stories, I can't help but wonder whether folks in the medical profession have changed or my friend's eyes have changed.

We can stop taking life for granted in stage four. We might drop through levels of feeling we have been gifted by life, letting go of the attitude that life owes us. I recall having a similar attitude at a Matthew Fox weekend workshop, where he encouraged us to find gratitude for a single breath. I knew immediately that gratitude for a single breath was not something I could easily access. It made sense to me and, at the same time, felt extremely foreign.

The following day around noon, I took a sip of water with my esophagus going into spasm. I could not breathe, and I was home alone. I was frightened and desperate as I began jumping up and down in the hope of disrupting the spasm. With no change, I ran out the front door of our home with no clue of where I was headed. The idea of running to a neighbor's house came and went. Suddenly, my esophagus relaxed. I sat on the outdoor step, still shaking from the ordeal, feeling not only gratitude but also a relief flushing my body. Loss does have a way of reminding us of that which deserves our gratitude as we watch a cherished person or thing fade away.

Of course, when life's demands roar in the here and now, gratitude may feel remote. That is when the "life owes me" attitude is likely to raise its voice. Emotional resiliency is easily compromised by a demanding urgency arising in us to flee or fix what is happening to us. When this urgency takes us hostage, it becomes much more difficult to cope with what life is presenting. Breathing into a pause, releasing any urgency to act, can leave us more accessible to more creative ways of responding to life's demands. The pause may open us to one single truth: "At this time, I'm not able to access any gratitude for the here and now." However, that keeps you in a relationship with the present that can be strengthened by asking, "What is this experience asking of me?"

When I recently suffered from a bout of Ménière's disease, symptoms of which include hearing loss and vertigo, I quickly responded with, "Life, you owe me." It took some time before I was willing to pause and allow myself to remain in a relationship with the here and now, where my symptoms were waiting for me. I finally got to the question while still feeling somewhat victimized by it: What are these symptoms asking of me? Slowly, voices from within began to surface: Listen to yourself. Listen to your limits. Listen to your adversarial relationship with aging. Although my left ear was losing its ability to hear, the inner voices were extremely audible.

STAGE FIVE:
Loyalty to the Moment

Around thirty years ago, my friend John, my son Jason, and I were visiting a Benedictine Monastery in Weston, Vermont. These monks are known for the quality of music they create as well as for offering their sanctuary to an immigrant Guatemalan family. Both accounts intrigued us. We stepped out of our vehicle and were prepared to walk across the parking lot to the gift shop. As my friend and my son made their way, I became fixated on a monk who was harvesting potatoes in the nearby field. My friend yelled back to me when he witnessed my pause. I assured him that I would join them momentarily. I remained in the grip of the vision of this monk attending to his task. For years, I wondered what captured my gaze that day while visiting the monastery.

Many years later, I came across the Orders of St. Benedict, which were his guidelines for monastic living. One of these was "loyalty to the moment." It caused me to pause and remember the monk I saw years ago working in the potato field. Had I witnessed a man working with loyalty to the here and now? What might it mean for anyone to work in such a manner?

Loyalty is living faithfully. We say that a loyal friend knows how to "be there" for us and is faithful to his word. We say that we are faithful to a friend or spouse when there is a commitment, a promise to accompany that person in good times and bad. The implication is that we will do our best to never allow ourselves to get excessively distracted from our commitment. Sometimes verbally, more often non-verbally, we know where or for whom our loyalty lives. If we're willing to get honest, we also know when loyalty from us or to us has been violated.

We know what it means to be loyal to others, but what about loyalty to the here and now? Let's look at how we can live faithfully to the moment:

- Loyalty to the here and now can only begin once we are aware of living in an unconscious and adversarial relationship with the moment.
- Once we can appreciate that that kind of relationship has taken care of us, we can begin to call off current hostilities and decide that the here and now is where we truly belong. We accept that the moment is life to be fully lived, including the delights and joys as well

as the defeats and hurts.

- We can get honest about our belonging to the here and now by admitting we will, on occasion, get excessively distracted in the past or future.
- Our loyalty is measured by our willingness to disrupt our distractions and return to where we belong.
- We remain mindful that we betray ourselves when we wander away from the here and now. That is, we sabotage the only place where we can be fully alive.
- We can strengthen our bond to the present by being aware of what we desire from it and by asking it: What are you asking of me? Such focuses keep the juices flowing from us to the present and back again.

Any talk about the here and now is ultimately a story about belonging. We are asked to surrender to more irony than we ever bargained for. The here and now is home, the time and place to love and be loved for joy, triumph, defeat, and suffering. Certainly, running feverishly into some allegedly exciting next moment, as well as dwelling on some memory of the past, stirring a heartfelt sentiment, are places to visit. However, if we allow, we can bet on being greeted, welcomed, and challenged in the here and now. We are both the host and the guest. There is always some part of us waiting in the moment for our welcome, some part that got pushed out in favor of a part of us we decided would make us look much better, at least to ourselves. Home is where the forgotten are remembered and where we can pause and settle into who we are, even when harvesting potatoes.

A MESSAGE FROM THE MOMENT

It may serve you to pause and pay attention to what
kind of relationship you have created with the Moment.
There are so many different ways to relate to the Moment.

In this moment, I would ask you to temporarily allow
your rational mind to fade into the background.
You can reclaim it in a bit,
but for now, welcome an old part of you.

A part of that was a dear friend: your imagination.
And allow the Moment to have a voice.
Let it tell you how it feels to be in a relationship with you
and in the hope that you might be receptive to what you hear.
Yes, let the voice of the Moment address you.
This may be the first time you allowed yourself to hear its voice.

"It's me, the Moment. Well, I've been waiting to let you
know my feelings about how you and I are doing.
I must say, I feel a bit used by you. You seem to fill me by trying
to prove something.
When I see you coming, you look very busy.
You attempt to prove that you're smart,
you prove that you're productive, that you have gifts.

"All this proving is about demonstrating that you deserve love.
All the while, I'm there believing that you deserve love,
believing that you're enough.
But you don't listen to me.
You treat me like I have nothing to offer you
and you don't even pause enough in my company
to ask what it is that I might be ready to give.

"I'm under the impression that when you're finished
pushing me out of the way,
you will simply shove the next moment in a similar fashion.
You live in such a frenzy that you have no idea
why I'm here or what I bring for you.
You don't know who I am.
When you keep me a stranger,
you remain a stranger to yourself.

"Maybe it's time for you to welcome me and
familiarize yourself with my offerings.
I am life, and when you receive me, you are also life.
Breathe slowly now,
lower your shoulders, open your closed fist,
fix a gentle gaze and imagine your heart settling
into the space I offer.
Now, feel the gifts of comfort and sweetness.

"You come to know the belonging that was always waiting for you.
You belong to the moment, the moment belongs to you,
you belong to life, and life belongs to you.
You may wander into my brothers and sisters,
the future and past.
However, I will be here, waiting for you,
welcoming your arrival again and again."

4: YOU CAN'T WIN THE GAME

"You can't win the game. You can only play it."

– *Bagger Vance*, The Legend of Bagger Vance

It was a while before I could understand and accept that I could not win the game of life. Our culture is obsessed with the illusion that we all can win. You just need the right education, the right networking, the right financial investments, and the right stuff to gain the upper hand. Of course, it means attaching ourselves to two illusions: first, that life is essentially understandable, and second, that we are all capable of such understanding. When failure happens, we either turn against life for having done awful things to us or condemn ourselves for being so inadequate.

TURNING AGAINST THE GAME AND OURSELVES

One way we turn against the mystery of life is to reduce our lives to whatever is practical. The concreteness of life lends itself to some sense of rightness or correctness. We can learn about personal hygiene, bringing beauty and order to an environment, purchasing and preparing healthy food, getting formally educated, acquiring a job, managing money, and acquiring social skills. Once we reduce life to these measurable items, we take comfort in the illusion of winning. Unfortunately, life doesn't appear to be content with being reduced to what brings us comfort. Natural disasters, loss, illness, oppression, and apparently unsolvable predicaments remind us of life's immensity.

The other option is to dare to bring more depth and meaning to the game. We can acknowledge the value of practical accomplishments and refuse to allow concrete matters to be the essential story of our lives. Hence, when it comes to expressions of life's mystery through simplicity, generosity, gratitude, humility, creativity, courage, and compassion, we must be ready to let go of winning. If we don't, we are inclined to turn against ourselves with accusations of stupidity, insensitivity, and lacking vision. These indictments suggest that the core of life's mysteries is penetrable, that we can shame ourselves into getting it right. If we are willing to let go of turning against life or ourselves, then we may allow ourselves to be loyal as the players we are.

THE GAME CAN GET YOU RIGHT

Allowing the game of life to get us right is a powerful spiritual mantra. It calls for a serious downsizing of the ego. Since most of our life experiences are out of our control, it makes sense to allow life to be mostly in control. When the game is allowed control, there's an opportunity for it to get us right. We return to who we were meant to be rather than pursuing who we thought we should be. Thomas Moore speaks about allowing life to teach: "Real strength of character shows itself in a willingness to let life sweep over us and burrow its way into us." As we allow life to "burrow its way into us," we take on lessons that endure throughout our lives rather than be satisfied with knowing how to operate the latest technological device.

Let's examine some ways we can allow the game to burrow, teaching us through ferocity and meekness, not always in equal measure:

- **Letting go.** Learning to let go of what is out of our control returns us to who we are, softening our allegiance to illusion and pretense. When we are less distracted by what is out of our control, we are more receptive to life's teachings.

- **Remain a student.** For life to get us right, we must allow it to teach us. This happens by being aware of attaching to contrived certainties that are organized to massage the ego. Remain curious. Hold your unknowing shamelessly. Do what you can to have faith that more will be revealed, especially when you feel lost. Always listen more than you speak. Stay close to the questions: Where in life are my actions yielding unsatisfactory results? Has complacency numbed my curiosity? What is my heart's longing? Is there a particular life pattern repeating itself, seeking my attention?

- **Getting support.** Adventuring into life's unknowns should not be done alone. We need viable support. The process is too big, and there is always the seduction of giving up and returning to something more parochial. We may feel overwhelmed to the point of needing others to carry us for a while. We can ask: Who in my life is a seeker? Who may be willing to accompany me? Am I willing to ask for their help? How might our collaboration be mutually beneficial?

- **Self-referenced but not personal.** Remaining self-referenced means staying focused on what we desire, love, feel, and value. Not allowing ourselves to take life too personally means recognizing that most experiences and choices reflect the human condition, your condition. Making mistakes in relationships, crafting a vocation, and living with more generosity and gratitude are much larger than who we are. We can acknowledge our shortcomings while also holding the immensity of the undertaking and the inevitability of some oversight.

- **Self-forgiveness.** We remain flawed, imperfect human beings, stumbling toward enlightenment. We will need to dare and risk stepping into the unknown. We must learn to forgive the stumbling and fumbling because, without forgiveness, we get preoccupied with self-abuse. We ignore the teacher and lessons that are shrouded by perseveration of criticism.

Striving to win at the game is a sure way to fail, and that may just be its greatest gift. It is typically failure that can help interrupt our fascination with winning. The hope is that life simply introduces its impenetrable mysteries over and over again until failure brings us to our knees with some interest in another option. At that point, we may have enough humility to become and remain devoted students of the game, allowing for its favorite pastime: teaching and allowing us to play soulfully.

THE CHALLENGE OF SELF-FORGIVENESS

"We all have some regrets as we age. Decisions that were too impetuous, mistakes that we believe could have been avoided, and people we unfortunately allowed to influence us. We can hold regrets softly as we see them as simply falling short of a perfect life. However, refusing to forgive ourselves can leave our aging stung by pessimism, self-contempt, and self-righteousness that finds others feeling not so deserving of forgiveness," explained Emma, reminding me of how much forgiving myself keeps me risk friendly and more curious about what life is asking of me.

"It does seem like quite an arduous task. I'm not sure if I or most folks even ask what forgiveness is and how to be up to offering it to ourselves," I pointed out.

"You're right. When the Church decided to make forgiveness something they and only they could offer, folks fell into a child's position, hoping that their transgressions would be wiped clean by a representative of the Church. It gave the clergy a great deal of power since they, as agents of God, were the only ones entitled to restore a person's goodness. The result has been that many of us are confused about what it means to reclaim the power to restore our personal worth," recounted Emma, her last sentence vibrating in the airways as if she was attempting to reach folks far removed from her office.

"It does seem like forgiveness is something only others can give us. If not a member of the clergy, then the offended party appears to have the power, whether they exercise it or not, to forgive us," I added, confident that Emma would elaborate.

"I don't even like the idea of pursuing forgiveness from another. If they decide to forgive, fine. However, my best wisdom is that the responsibility lies with us. It's up to us to get straight with ourselves by reclaiming our essential worth. Give more thought to the nature of self-forgiveness and what might get in your way, inhibiting the self-forgiveness process. We need to learn that winning at the game of life is not possible. People often talk about 'being in the zone.' That means playing well, right?" Emma confirmed, squinting her eyes as if the light of this issue possessed an intensity of illumination.

"Yes, being in the zone does typically mean that good things are happening," I replied.

"In that case, then, nothing places us more in the zone than self-forgiveness. When we trust we will do our best to forgive ourselves, we're much more willing to play the game and not sit on the sidelines," offered Emma, inspiring me to get clearer about the value of self-forgiveness.

I began my inquiry by looking at the word *forgive* to shed some light on what happens when we are forgiving. The prefix *for* comes from German, meaning "away." We can say that the word *forgive* might mean "away give" or "give away (someone's) wrongdoing or transgressions." Giving away suggests we are letting go of the infraction in question, including any cursing we leveled against the offender over what was committed. Genuine forgiveness entails seeing and honoring the person's essential goodness.

Most of us were taught that forgiveness happens between people. Either we are forgiving someone, or someone is forgiving us. Certainly, when we authentically forgive or are forgiven by someone, there are numerous possible advantages to restoring the relationship. However, the same is true of self-forgiveness. Many possible benefits come from learning to forgive ourselves. Even the focus of working on forgiving ourselves guides our attention in an honorable direction. Let's begin by looking at why it may be so difficult to make the offering of forgiveness to ourselves.

WHAT GETS IN THE WAY?

There are several significant impediments to growing a facility for self-forgiveness:

We are taught that forgiveness is something we can only receive from others. This relinquishes control over our worth to someone else. It is easy for authority figures to fall prey to framing forgiveness as something they either offer or withhold. And so, we hold the belief that they have more power to modify a subordinate's behavior. This strategy may have short-term effectiveness but shows no substantial capacity to instill certain values that positively guide a child's actions.

Invalidation of self-forgiveness. Self-forgiveness is often described as disingenuous. It is suggested that forgiving ourselves is accompanied by a cavalier attitude aimed simply at making us feel better about ourselves. In other words, we are only attempting to mitigate guilt and remorse for our benefit. Hence our insistence that the only valid forgiveness comes from the person we offended or a religious representative. In either case, responsibility and control over our goodness lie in the hands of others. To be self-forgiving doesn't mean we take a cavalier attitude toward our behavior, dismissing the gravity of what we have done. We can gradually move into deepening levels of self-forgiveness accompanied by regret and remorse.

Allegedly protecting against future wrongdoing. If we withhold forgiving ourselves, the thinking goes, then we have more control over preventing some future occurrence of unacceptable behavior. I often refer to this strategy as "Bad Self-Parenting." It didn't work when our parents did it to us, and it doesn't work when we do it to ourselves.

Refusal to accept personal limits. This is a popular impediment to self-forgiveness. It is the refusal to accept the weakness or short-sightedness that gave rise to some impropriety. Rather than forgive ourselves, we cling to the vision of a more idyllic consideration of who we could be. This obstacle is typically driven by arrogance, as we are always supposed to be better. The idea of arrogance driving our resistance to forgive ourselves came home to me one day while working with Emma. I detailed something I had done for which I struggled to forgive myself. Emma gently looked at me and said, "Do you believe you should have been bigger?" I lost my breath. It felt like too much truth to swallow all at once. Once I was able to find my voice, I blurted out, "Of course I believe I should have been bigger!" I could see that forgiving myself was asking for a measure of humility which I knew was not yet in my grasp; I resisted accepting my limits.

Confirmation of some self-diminishing way in which we already see ourselves. Rather than forgive ourselves, we gather more data in support of viewing ourselves as damaged goods. One alleged benefit is that it may support us to be risk averse. Given our alleged defect, we consider it foolish to take on any measure of risk.

BENEFITS OF SELF-FORGIVENESS

If we are willing to become apprentices of self-forgiveness, the benefits are likely to be numerous:

It gives us responsibility for and control over forgiveness and our essential worth. Restoring our relationship with ourselves is our responsibility. If we violate our values, hurting others in the process, it is our responsibility to do what needs to be done to move back into integrity.

It confirms our humanity. Self-forgiveness has the power to interrupt aspirations of perfectionism. Perfectionism is an attempt to eclipse the human condition. It is an assault on our humanity. When we are willing to forgive ourselves, we are more accepting of our humanity and willing to work with it rather than striving to win a game that can't be won.

It supports learning how to make mistakes. Knowing how to make mistakes is an art form. Self-forgiveness allows us to feel regret and remorse before moving on to respond creatively to the blunder. The creative energies begin to coalesce when we substitute curiosity in place of ridiculing ourselves. Curiosities include: What part of me made this mistake? Did I succ-umb to some seduction that resulted in me stepping away from what I truly value? What was I attempting to accomplish? What or who needed to be further considered? What is the mistake asking of me? What may obstruct deeper learning? With whom would it benefit me to explore these questions?

It helps diminish self-righteousness. When we demand living by a higher standard, self-forgiveness can be difficult to come by. It is also likely that the attachment to some higher standard engenders a sense of self-righteousness as we strive to be who we should be rather than who we are. Being mindful of self-righteousness has the power to restore us to our common humanity.

It helps us become more risk friendly. We fundamentally do not fear taking risks. We fear the abusive treatment we will likely inflict upon ourselves if a risk yields unfavorable consequences. The more we trust that we will do our best to issue self-forgiveness when there are adverse results, the more likely we are to take risks.

It supports the deepening of our capacity to learn. Learning suggests we are stepping onto unfamiliar terrain. We are novices to new material. Self-forgiveness issues pervasive compassion, affording us a new level of grace as we embrace unknowing. Such grace offers suppleness as we stumble into getting some concept wrong, allowing for movement forward rather than getting stuck seeing ourselves as wrong.

It benefits others. We are not the only beneficiaries of self-forgiveness. A willingness to learn about forgiving ourselves is tantamount to learning how to be more fully alive. When taking a risk is less of an opportunity to enact self-admonishment, we explore more, appreciating the opportunity to go somewhere new. We likely see more, engage more, and give and receive more. Perseverating in the wake of our transgressions is replaced by a renewed readiness for involvement. We allow what and whom we love to be witnessed.

THE ART OF SELF-FORGIVENESS

As discussed above, we are taught that forgiveness is something we give to others and receive from others. Folks who are in some way offended, hurt, or violated by us are allegedly in control of whether or not we are deserving of forgiveness. This leaves us virtually out of control regarding the role of forgiveness in our lives. For example, someone consumed by revenge may be a significant impediment to our experience of being forgiven.

The result is that forgiveness from ourselves becomes confusing and arduous. Let's look at some steps that can yield a budding aptitude for self-forgiveness.

STEPS TO SELF-FORGIVENESS

Making self-forgiveness normal and a priority. Forgiving ourselves will not happen magically. It will more likely take place because we make it an important task to attend to. I often hear, "I haven't forgiven myself for some situation." I typically respond, "I hear that you haven't forgiven yourself, and can you tell me what you are doing to yourself instead of forgiveness?" The common responses include stories describing themselves as depraved, inadequate, sinful, and unworthy. The key here is to be curious about what the attachment to being self-effacing is supposed to offer. For example, what might be learned by focusing on the attachment rather than the alleged accusation that there is something wrong with you?

Identifying the purpose of ongoing belittlement. With only a little curiosity, it becomes clear that the purpose of withholding forgiveness and replacing it with ongoing self-repudiation is the belief that such harsh treatment will prevent the unacceptable behavior from being repeated. Of course, such cruelty does not evoke some profound shift in character. Continuing to prioritize self-forgiveness means being willing to interrupt the self-deprecating stories we create and accepting that they are not a very effective method for staying straight with our values.

Accepting and talking about feelings of remorse, regret, guilt, and shame due to violating your values. This step suggests the importance of knowing our values and when they have been breached. When people complain and object to your behavior, this doesn't mean you did something wrong. Wrong action is determined by our values and not by the disapproval of others. We can use the disapproval of others to check whether we acted in opposition to one of our values. If we have not violated one of our values, then we need to exercise enough resilience to sustain self-acceptance when being disapproved of by others.

Moving out of a fixation on self-incrimination. It is important to process what happened to enlarge our vision of how we came to make the choice we did. Some questions that can be helpful include: How did I come to believe that the action carried out was not a violation of my values? Did the action reflect the result of two competing values, with one being sacrificed? Were there intervening variables I was not aware of? Is there some understanding of my motivation that I can cultivate in hindsight?

Restitution and/or making amends. Is there some compensation to be offered to the injured party in the way of service, reparation, or replacement of damaged property? Sometimes, making amends can be helpful in support of forgiving ourselves. An amend is an apology or expression of regret accompanied by a commitment to refrain from the adverse behavior in question. An amend is not offered if it would create greater harm to either the injured party or the person making amends.

Accepting that playing the game fully alive means making mistakes. This calls for a level of humility, allowing us to be more accepting of our limits and letting go of perfectionistic aspirations. Striving to be mistake-free is an insult to the human condition and who we are as humans. I like seeing mistakes as my willingness to accept the invitation to be fully alive. My goal is to take on the responsibility of forgiving myself, remembering the ego's ongoing investment in being bigger than my mistakes.

Ask for help. It can be very important to turn to a friend, mentor, counselor, or clergy member we trust to guide us toward authentic self-forgiveness. The helper must not attempt to minimize what we did just to make us feel more cheerful. Nor should the helper be prone to shame us. Helpers need to offer the kind of support that leads us to hold a larger understanding of what we did while assisting us in interrupting any perfectionism. When it is difficult for me to summon self-forgiveness, I remember Emma's words: "Did you think that you were supposed to be bigger?" Of course, the answer is "yes." And then, I'm staring down the barrel of an insidious arrogance. Quite often, the resistance to forgive travels in tandem with an attachment to being exceptional. Nothing can be more useful about helping us accept ourselves as ordinary human beings than making a mistake and committing to an offering of self-forgiveness.

Being unskilled at self-forgiveness can leave us dependent on others for our self-worth, to being risk averse, haunted by guilt and shame, trapped in self-loathing, and condemned to excessive timidity where the hope is that making mistakes will be minimized. Ultimately, becoming more effective at self-forgiveness is a way for us to remain responsible for self-worth. It is also a large welcome to our humanity as we release perfectionistic aspirations, attending to the tasks of inner reconciliation and being an ordinary person.

Making peace with ourselves is not a self-absorbed activity. As elders, we can live with more courage when devotionally moving toward self-forgiveness. A risk that might have unfavorable consequences is no longer paralyzing, as we can anticipate moving toward self-forgiveness. Such freedom can yield more depth and meaning in our relationships.

When, as elders, we are not defending a self-concept pummeled by guilt and self-incrimination, we become more generous with offering compassion to others. Forgiveness possesses a heart-opening quality that tempers resentment and vindictiveness, allowing us to be more receptive to seeking reconciliation with others. As we strive less for perfection, we discover a growing acceptance of the limits and shortcomings of others. There is an abiding honoring of the human condition reflected by our own lives and the lives of others. The willingness to be forgiving of ourselves allows us as elders to be lived by life rather than ruminating about how to strategically win—all the while remembering that the game holds the trump card of death.

5: The Power of Being and the Power of Becoming

"Profound truth, like the vocabulary of virtue, eludes formulation. It quickly becomes rigid, gives way to abstraction or cliché. But put a spiritual insight to a story, an experience, a face; describe where it anchors in the ground of your being; and it will change you in the telling and others in the listening."

– Krista Tippett

Emma was particularly interested in talking about the Power of Being, suggesting that it guides the soulful path to elderhood. I began to appreciate how our conversations led me to further consideration of a path I deeply wanted to understand and follow.

"I find myself concerned about a loss of power as I grow older, which I feel a bit embarrassed saying," I admitted, feeling assured that Emma would handle my embarrassment with care. I was curious to see how she would address this issue of power.

"I understand. There is a loss of power, a loss of the Power of Becoming. What most folks who are aging don't realize is that there is an immense opportunity to acquire more of the Power of Being," Emma pointed out, her voice carrying a flavor of sympathy for those of us unaware of how much the Power of Being is available.

I responded, "Being and Becoming: Did they originate in Western civilization around 500 BC in Greece? As I recall, there were two schools of thought about cosmology or the study of what is real. One school of thought suggested that reality was ever unfolding or becoming transitory and advancing. This was referred to as the non-static nature of reality. If I'm not mistaken, the thinkers representing a Becoming cosmology included Thales, Xenophanes, Democritus, Anaximenes, and, later, Aristotle. One of the famous pre-Socratic philosophers was Heraclitus, who claimed, 'No man steps in the same river twice, for it is not the same river, and he's not the same man.'"

"The Being perspective of reality was represented by Parmenides, Anaximander, Anaxagoras, and Plato," I added, delighted in recalling my early days of immersion in the history of philosophy. "Their view accounted for reality as possessing a certain constant, not susceptible to change and existing beyond the senses."

"Rather than looking at Being and Becoming as cosmological perspectives, I suggest that you consider them from a psychological perspective in terms of bringing power to our choices. Try looking at them as psychological contraries sharing some commonalities," Emma encouraged, leaving me feeling enlivened about the Power of Being naturally evolving for me if I pay attention to living a self-examined life.

I left Emma's ready to distinguish between these two forms of Power. I began to see that both belonging and networking were social phenomena. However, Belonging calls on emotional energies that have more depth, are more sustainable, and are reflective of the Power of Being. Where networking has some particular goal to advance, it is transitory and, therefore, listed under the Power of Becoming. Maybe the early Greek influence can be seen in the items listed under the Power of Being, as they seem to have more sustainability and less susceptibility to the influence of their zeitgeist.

I was reminded of something mythologist Michael Meade wrote regarding the two arcs of life: "While following the first arc, we 'make a life' and learn to make our way in the day-to-day world." Thus, the Power of Becoming energizes the first arc of life. Meade goes on to say, "The second arc of life involves an involution or turning within to seek self-knowledge and develop greater self-awareness. This inward arc depends on reflection, remembering, and becoming aware of the core pattern of one's soul and the inherent purpose of one's life. The inner arc bends toward things eternal; it involves the dream of one's life and the life of one's dreams. This is the arc of growing consciousness, genuine calling, and potentiality of spiritual fulfillment."

I could see that the Power of Becoming animates the first arc and moves up and outward in alignment with cultural expectations of what is important. It helps us "make a life." The Power of Being moves inward in the direction of our depths. This process requires a modification of the ego.

I returned to Emma's much clearer about the difference between these two Powers.

"I can see just how much our culture is hooked on the Power of Becoming," I began, hoping Emma would pick up on my implied enthusiasm for the Power of Being, since it was bringing more hope as the Power of Becoming waned.

"Absolutely. Religions, schools, other social organizations, and the norms of the typical American family teach and model the Power of Becoming. The problem is that life cannot be understood or deeply lived from this Power alone. Our nomenclature is limited to the Power of Becoming any time the word *power* is spoken or written. We think, talk, dream, and act as if the Power of Becoming is the only way to relate to our lived experience," Emma added with a note of condemnation.

"I'm reminded that an ancient definition of the word *power* is 'to be able.' When restricted to the Power of Becoming, we run the risk of not being able to be guided by our inner landscape," I added.

Emma leaped from her seat, pulled a book from her shelf, and began to read: "'I stopped in the middle of that building, and I saw—sky. I saw the things that I love in this world: the work and the food and time to sit and smoke. And I looked at the pen and said to myself, what the hell am I grabbing for? Why am I trying to become what I don't want to be? What am I doing in this office, making a contemptuous, begging fool of myself when all I want is out there, waiting for me the minute I say I know who I am! Why can't I say that, Willy?' That's from Arthur Miller's *Death of a Salesman*, capturing the kind of alienation that ensues when we settle for the Power of Becoming," Emma explained, not attempting to conceal her contempt for cultural invitations to get lost in the Power of Becoming.

I returned to Emma's, eager to share the writing I had done regarding distinguishing features of these two expressions of power and what I believe happens when we only employ the Power of Becoming:

The Power of Being	The Power of Becoming
Internal Focus	External focus
Living a self-examined life	Living a life examining economic and political conditions
Tracking the pulse of one's emotional & spiritual life	Tracking social and economic opportunity
Valuing feeling vulnerable, leading to living with more heart and more courage	Valuing ego strength, leading to greater efficacy & executive functioning
Prioritizing collaboration & co-creativity	Prioritizing competition

Welcoming personal wounds & gifts of the wounds	Welcoming personal strengths & talents
Valuing living authentically	Valuing adaption to external norms & expectations
Valuing the development of a deep sense of belonging	Valuing an ability to network
Able to employ surrender as an expression of power	Able to employ willfulness as an expression of power
Valuing the development of emotional intimacy	Valuing casual friendships and membership in professional associations
Desiring mindfulness and equanimity as outcomes	Desiring a fulfilling occupation and solvent finances as desired outcomes
Prioritizing emotional intelligence and wisdom	Prioritizing abstract & practical intelligence
Prioritizing integrity	Prioritizing a positive reputation
Prioritizing workshops and training focused on emotional intelligence and spiritual development	Prioritizing formal education
Inclined toward unconditional love	Inclined toward conditional love
Employing power through surrender	Employing power through acts of will

It became increasingly obvious that attempting to live life from one form of power could be disastrous. It would also be natural to scurry about attempting to fill in the holes left when trying to create a life with the use of the Power of Becoming alone. We can see these strategies as compensations for the loss of the Power of Being.

COMPENSATIONS

It is natural to compensate when attempting to live with only one form of power. However, this compensatory move possesses some unfortunate consequences. Let's explore some of these unfavorable outcomes.

Compensation for little or no interior vision. When our interior worlds are defined as being off-limits, there is a propensity to exaggerate our external focus, getting lost in conventional beliefs and values. We can no longer guide our lives through intuition, imagination, and heart. Integrity is seriously compromised.

Compensation for low emotional intelligence. When this occurs, cognitive or intellectual activity is aggrandized. The results include low self-awareness, limited capacity to collaborate and communicate effectively, diminished ability to exercise empathy, and confusion about emotions leading to an impaired ability to generate emotional intimacy accompanied by unconsciously biased thinking.

Compensation for feeling vulnerable. This compensation is expressed as an exaggerated persona of bravado often accompanied by rampant ambition and, when pushed, unbridled attempts at domination.

Compensation for genuine belonging. There is a tendency to obsessively make varied acquisitions in an attempt to fill the emptiness created by the absence of real connections to others. In the absence of belonging, it can be easy to fall prey to collecting admirers and fans while numbing the self through the abuse of food, pharmaceuticals, alcohol, and street drugs.

Compensation for feeling helpless. When the exercise of will is the only expression of power, we are not able to effectively navigate what is out of our control. We are not able to live life on life's terms, asserting delusions of control, distortions about one's limits, and perfectionistic demands of oneself and others.

"I like what you're saying about these two Powers. We have all been acculturated with the Power of Becoming as if it is the only Power. The patriarchy then decided that only white males are entitled to the Power of Becoming," Emma pointed out, her jaw tightening and her eyes expanding, suggesting an unqualified focus.

"Well, thank God for feminism! It has helped women access the Power of Becoming. Those women paved a path for my daughters and granddaughter," I added, feeling grateful.

"Without a doubt, those early feminists cracked open the Boys' Club, and there's still plenty of work to do. Sometimes, I regret that those original heroines didn't see that they were entitled to the Power of Being. It's too easy to become myopic when viewing what the culture holds sacred," concluded Emma with an unbridled passion that seemed ready to address the women of America.

"Are you suggesting that the goal for liberated women is not to become like men?"

"Sure, the goal is to become a whole person, holding both expressions of power," reassured Emma, leaving me with more clarity about how both genders can be seduced by the Power of Becoming.

"I see how women protested not being able to access the Power of Becoming. I was quite active in the mythopoetic men's movement, and I believe that our purpose was to invite men to open themselves to the Power of Being," I suggested, making no effort to conceal my regret that many men may not have gotten the message.

"It would have been difficult for men to insist that they be entitled to the Power of Being when the culture doesn't view that as a worthwhile pursuit. And it is probably safe to say that the cultural definition of manhood was heavily imbued with the features of the Power of Becoming. Desiring the Power of Being often places manhood in a precarious spot," Emma added, resulting in me feeling thankful that she could appreciate the challenges facing men regarding power.

"It appears that both genders only desire the Power of Becoming. I recall some feminists claiming that the men in the men's movement were trying to secure more socioeconomic and political power—that is, the Power of Becoming. I can safely vouch for how much these men wanted to learn how to live with more heart and learn to serve with that heart. We didn't call it the Power of Being, but that's exactly what it was. No one was attempting to strategize how he might make a buck," I asserted, my anger more than obvious.

"Yes, that's what you guys were up to, and it's great that some men stayed with it, like the men who attend the Connecticut Men's Gathering. Of course, it is easy to see why retirement can hurl a man into a crisis of meaning. As the Power of Becoming begins to wane in the absence of any integration of the Power of Being, it won't be clear why life is worth living with no real source of power to turn to," Emma sadly expressed, with the truth underlying men's concerns with aging entering the room.

"I think we're saying that the more folks allow for both forms of power, the soulful path to elderhood becomes more accessible," I added.

"It is critical to make the Power of Being more visible, more understandable, and more lived. It will serve men and women as well as those who do not fit into a gender binary. A sacred path to elderhood depends upon it," Emma affirmed, leaving me once again thankful for being in the presence of the voice of an authentic elder who seemed to hold the elder path equally for all genders.

A BLESSING FOR THE POWER OF BEING

There are ancient rivals named Becoming and Being.
Even if you have not thought about Becoming or talked about it,
your body knows Becoming as doing.
You get educated, pursue occupational goals, you achieve,
you create a home, you pay bills, and rake leaves in Autumn.

Without a great deal of consideration,
you give Becoming the power to hold your essential worth.
And rightly so—you build, you generate, you create,
you fix, you teach, and maybe you heal.
However, there comes a time when the weight of the soul's
sacredness asks for more.

When does striving bring fatigue to the soul?
Have you allowed yourself to feel how lost you
may become amid the pile of actions?
Can you pause and wonder who you might be when you
crawl out from that pile?
How many successes will be enough to confirm that you are enough?

If you know the emptiness of Becoming,
then trust that knowing.
Becoming has its place;
it's not enough to birth meaning and depth.
You know the whispers of Being
when you give yourself permission to nap.
There is Being in the tenderness of deserving rest.
Deservedness is the cradle of Being.

It puts proving to rest.
Proving is so easily laced through all expressions of Becoming.
Proving hides itself behind the veils of being
ambitious, productive, creative, and responsible.
Proving possesses an insatiable hunger.

We prove that we are enough, deserving of love.
We prove we are worthy of forgiveness regarding
our last transgression.
We attempt to prove we merit redemption for having loved poorly.
These strivings are of no avail;
they simply place us
on the mountain with Sisyphus—forever incomplete.

Being is knocking on the door of your soul
when urgency subsides, when doing loses its tenacity,
and the next best thing to do fades behind the
shadow of an incandescent light cast by the joy
of what is happening now, no matter how simple.
The gift of Being is a love asking for no proof.

6: Promises

We come to know the meaning of promises when, beyond some aspiration of the ego, we promise to give ourselves to that which truly matters. Such a promise is made to ourselves, to life, and to the gods.

I returned to Emma's excited to be talking about promises as if it were a very new idea. In a way, they were.

"I came across the poem entitled 'Stopping by Woods on a Snowy Evening' by Robert Frost. The last verse keeps calling to me. I can't get it out of my mind," I announced, excited to share with Emma, whom I imagined had heard much of this in the past, yet was still able to lean in with curiosity and enthusiasm.

"Well, I vaguely recall that poem. Can you paraphrase the last verse?"

"I have a copy with me; I'd like to read the whole thing to you. I strongly feel it points toward the soulful path to elderhood," I continued, pulling out a copy of the poem:

> Whose woods these are I think I know.
> His house is in the village though;
> He will not see me stopping here
> To watch his woods fill up with snow.
>
> My little horse must think me queer
> To stop without a farmhouse near

Between the woods and frozen lake
The darkest evening of the year.

He gives his harness bells a shake
To ask if there is some mistake.
The only other sound's the sweep
Of easy wind and downy flake.

The woods are lovely, dark, and deep.
But I have promises to keep,
And miles to go before I sleep,
And miles to go before I sleep.

"There's a touching simplicity in the words, something about a man and his horse, his ability to take the time to witness beauty on a snowy evening. Then, there are these promises and so many miles to go. I want to hear more about the impact the promises are having on you," Emma requested as she sat back, striking a receptive pose.

"I immediately thought of promises taking the place of purposes. Maybe purpose fits the vision of a younger person with allegedly more life ahead than behind. A purpose also seems to be mostly about the vision of a sizable goal. A promise is palpable. It is intended to be felt and lived. An old definition of the word *promise* is 'to send forth.' A promise seems to be relational: there is a sender and a receiver. Even if we make a promise to ourselves, there's still a sender and a receiver," I explained in the hope that Emma could feel the spirit of promises running through me.

"I hear the more embodied nature of a promise as opposed to a purpose," agreed Emma, her voice trailing off, waiting to receive more from me.

"Yes, to say 'I have a purpose,' even if it somehow involves others, is a great deal about me. A promise seems to imply a recipient. There's so much about our understanding of the soul that implies being relational. The poem suggests that a man is experiencing an aesthetic moment, which is absolutely fine, and yet he must not linger. He has promises to keep and miles to go before he sleeps. I certainly see the soulful path as affording opportunity for the appreciation of beauty while not surpassing the devotion to keeping promises before death descends," I explained, feeling the words dropping deeper within me, calling me to make some promise to life.

"Do you see promises being made mostly to other people?" Emma asked.

"That is certainly how we conventionally think of promises. However, I really enjoy personifying life by making promises to it," I explained, hoping Emma would not see me as excessively romantic.

"These promises to life suggest a vital way for elders to serve life. A soulful path to elderhood must be about service. From that perspective, 'miles to go' depicts the numerous offerings that an elder can make to life before it's time to take a more relaxed posture," added Emma, leaving me feeling very understood.

I left our conversation wanting to clarify some of the promises that are fitting for an elder to make to life.

SOME ELDER PROMISES

- I promise to surrender to something larger than myself.
- I promise to work toward holding the belief that life owes me nothing.
- I promise to continue living a self-examined life.
- I promise to bring compassion to what I discover about myself.
- I promise to employ my gifts in support of the empowerment of young people.

- I promise to live my questions with the faith that more will be revealed.
- I promise to exercise my discernment in promoting what is truly sustainable.
- I promise to remain curious about what life is asking of me.
- I promise to pay attention to where I separate myself unnecessarily.
- I promise to return to unity consciousness whenever possible.
- I promise to pass on the encouragement and knowledge that was given to me.
- I promise to exercise the discernment needed to identify who truly wants my offerings.
- I promise to serve.
- I promise to maintain an open and curious relationship with ambiguity.

When I returned to Emma's, I read my list of Elder Promises.

"I like them a lot. What about the promise to remain a meaning-maker?" suggested Emma, her desire to collaborate making it easier for me to welcome more breath.

"I hear the importance of aging and remaining a meaning-maker. I'll add it to the list. Culture seems to ascribe meaning-making to folks who are at the height of their careers, building something, making deals, teaching, healing, and generally producing. I'm assuming that is the reason so many people go into a crisis of meaning when retiring," I offered, feeling a loosening of my jaw and an increased acceptance of my aging—or maybe I was just seeing aging as appropriate.

"Surely, our society does not attribute the power to make meaning to older folks. You have suggested much of the reason for that can be seen in your distinction between the Power of Becoming and the Power of Being. Meaning is often perceived as spinning off the Power of Becoming. Aging or retirement is a grand opportunity to welcome the Power of Being into your life, allowing it to be a source of meaning-making," Emma explained, her tone suggesting that the topic was directly in her wheelhouse.

"I didn't see it originally, but the promises I outlined are a vivid depiction of the Power of Being. I'm very aware of how much is lost when restricting ourselves to the Power of Becoming, which is very much focused on clarity and generating answers. Doesn't some writer make a case for ambiguity being critical in a quest for meaning?" I wondered.

"Yes, James Hollis makes a case for a relationship with ambiguity being a prerequisite for making meaning. It's easy to see when we consider that what truly gives meaning to our lives is all steeped in ambiguity. Love, freedom, courage, generosity, authenticity, devotion, and wisdom, to name just a few, are all imbued with uncertainty," Emma added, helping me appreciate that someone had sung the praises of ambiguity.

"I feel clearer about the challenge of remaining a meaning-maker and how aging need not impede the process. It helps me if I give it more thought and, maybe, write about what might get in the way of having an open relationship with ambiguity," I said, realizing how much writing helped clarify an inquiry and had me feeling a bit presumptuous about writing about things I did not yet understand.

As I drove away from Emma's, I kept thinking that there was something about unresolved trauma that very well might be an issue when attempting to relate to ambiguity.

7: SEEKING MEANING BEYOND TRAUMA

"If there is meaning in life at all, then there must be meaning in suffering.
Suffering is an ineradicable part of life, even as fate and death.
Without suffering and death human life cannot be complete."

– Viktor Frankl

For many, the search for genuine meaning remains a desirous lifelong pursuit. There are many expressions of meaning. How do we know when our lives can be characterized as meaningful? On a very fundamental level, searching for meaning places your life in a context of meaning. That is, you know what it means to lose meaning and to reacquire it.

An old definition of the word *meaning* is "to name." When we name ourselves, we are attributing meaning to our lives, and retirement can be a time when we simply do not know how to name ourselves. We can name ourselves as lovers of apple turnovers or as someone dedicated to supporting others in maximizing their human potential. The more devotion we get behind the name and the more the name points to serving something larger than ourselves, the greater the depth and breadth of the meaning created. We might say that the richness of a meaningful life reflects what truly matters. Some ways to lean into the direction of creating meaning include identifying what you desire from life, acknowledging what life is asking of you, knowing your gifts and how they might best serve, and knowing and living what you love.

Being able to generate meaning that offers direction and fulfillment depends on an open and workable relationship with ambiguity or uncertainty, as well as taking action that consummates the vision we hold. The credibility of the previous statement is affirmed when we are willing to get honest about the mystery, unpredictability, and insecurity of life, as well as so many of the dynamics that generate real meaning. I was reminded of Emma's words regarding how much ambiguity is carried by what truly matters. Some of these dynamics shrouded in ambiguity include love, freedom, justice, courage, emotional intimacy, wisdom, and compassion.

Many Indigenous cultures Initiate young people into the mystery of life through a rite of passage, which anthropologists refer to as the ritual of the Mysterium Tremendum or Great Mystery. We continue to insist that the delusions of the right education, right bank account, right job, right spouse, and right neighborhood will make life certain, predictable, and secure. Those things can create a measure of comfort but can't strip life of its mystery.

In a culture that denies the kind of relationship with ambiguity that is capable of generating meaning, distractions are everywhere. The attachment to immediate gratification, needing to impress, addiction, arrested development, and hubris can easily block the pursuit of meaning. However, early trauma, especially complex trauma involving ongoing violations of a child's physical, sexual, or emotional boundaries or some premature loss, can substantially inhibit one's ability to generate authentic meaning. Trauma places the nervous system on alert for possible threats to safety. Being driven by a hijacked amygdala, children may move into adulthood vigilantly patrolling the environment in survival mode.

LITERALIZED OR LOST

My work with early trauma has shown that there are at least two significant ways in which trauma can become an impediment to being comfortable relating to ambiguity. The first group I identify as "literalized," as they move away from ambiguity by reducing their experience to concrete information gathered by the five senses. The second group I identify as "lost," as they wander in ambiguity, unable to bring meaning through real action. Let's first look more closely at the former.

LITERALIZING THE AMBIGUOUS

This group of survivors seems to have the predisposition to gather information in concrete terms via the five senses. Therefore, they can be defined as concrete learners. For more on concrete learners, I suggest reviewing Anthony Gregorc's Learning Typology Model. Meaning is attributed to what is seen, heard, touched, tasted, and smelled. Negotiating emotions, values, abstract principles, and diverse beliefs can be challenging. Black-and-white thinking places abstract considerations in neat boxes, missing the nuances of lived experiences.

As tolerance and acceptance for the unknown wane, so does the need for immediate information increase. Because these adults were likely abused by family authority figures, any lack of clarity expressed by a contemporary authority figure will be immediately called into question. Typically, there is a receptivity to any charismatic leader exuberantly announcing opinions, regardless of how factual they are. As a result, conspiracy theories become extremely appealing.

In a recent article in *Psychology Today*, Dr. David Ludden points out that, in a confused world, people seek answers that comfort them and fit into their worldview—answers that offer a sense of control and security as well as an opportunity to maintain a positive self-image aligning themselves with those who passionately claim to possess the truth. A history of complex trauma greatly amplifies the need to feel comforted by a particular worldview, to have a sense of control and security, as well as a positive self-image. This makes folks who suffered from complex trauma especially receptive to conspiracy theories, as the black and white thinking of childhood continues.

The consequence of not being able to cope with ambiguity is captured in the following quote by James Hollis: "Living with ambiguity, not being too attached to the old 'certainties,' and learning what life needs to tell us whether or not we think we are up to it are, frankly, the only ways to grow, become more capacious, live a larger journey." When we are threatened by the ambiguity of "what life needs to tell us" we sacrifice living a larger journey.

When the ability to hold ambiguity and learn from it is compromised, several significant consequences result, leaving us living a small journey:

1) There is a rigid attachment to black-and-white thinking with little tolerance for the gray areas of life. The most significant aspects of life come in gray: justice, love, freedom, responsibility, compassion, courage, integrity, morality, and a mature spirituality, to name a few.

2) Because the above life experiences can be described as ambiguous meaning-makers, any adverse response to ambiguity can seriously mitigate the ability to create meaning in one's life.

3) It becomes challenging to live life on life's terms as life tends to unfold ambiguously by way of mystery and unpredictability.

4) Thinking in reductive terms of right and wrong tends to seriously weaken a capacity to work with diverse beliefs, values, and needs.

5) The essential ingredients of curiosity, wonder, and imagination that support a comfort with the unknown are muted. They are suspended in favor of maintaining reliable surveillance of the environment. In his book, *The Body Keeps the Score*, Bessel van der Kolk addresses the impact chronic trauma has on imagination: "When people are compulsively and constantly pulled back into the past, to the last time they felt intense involvement and deep emotions, they suffer from a failure of imagination, a loss of mental flexibility. Without imagination there is no hope, no chance to envision a better future, no place to go, no goal to reach."

6) Clear responses to the dynamics occurring in an intimate emotional relationship are compromised. In the absence of immediate and concrete answers to ambiguous emotional issues, participants feel overwhelmed.

MAKING PEACE WITH AMBIGUITY

Making peace with ambiguity for adults who suffer from chronic developmental trauma will call for patience and receiving viable support. The following are several recommendations:

1) Learn to regulate your nervous system by first being able to distinguish a regulated nervous system from an unregulated one. Indicators of dysregulation include increased heart rate, shallow breathing, agitation, sweaty palms, increased muscle tension, becoming aggressive or withdrawn, an inability to identify what one

needs, and extreme thinking (everyone/no one, never/ always, etc.).

2) It is critical to interrupt any shaming or ridiculing thoughts about your unregulated nervous system. It can help to recall that an unregulated nervous system once assisted you in your survival of childhood.

3) Physical movement by exercising or taking a walk can help interrupt an incapacitating reaction.

4) Focus on your external sense, especially sight and touch. Visualize the colors, shapes, and textures in your immediate environment. Focus on internal sensations such as pulsation above the eyes, tight gut, increased heart rate, tense jaw, and flushed cheeks.

5) Upon reaching a measure of calm, acknowledge that you are learning to face ambiguity and its accompanying tension while letting yourself know that you are safe.

6) Give yourself the option of a physical boundary to support the feeling of safety. For example, you might leave a room where contentious feelings are escalating.

7) Close your eyes and visualize yourself in a place where you feel comfortably free, courageous, or intimate. Hold the image for a minute or so, and then begin to track your internal sensations.

8) Speak to trusted others about your apprenticeship with ambiguity. Tell them about the challenges and accomplishments alike.

9) Most somatic therapies can be quite helpful. I especially recommend Somatic Experiencing and EMDR.

10) With the right support and a measure of grace, the concrete learner may be able to find enough safety to be guided by the words of Rainer Maria Rilke: "Be patient toward all that is unsolved in your heart and try to love the questions themselves ... Live the questions now.

Perhaps you will then gradually, without noticing it, live along some distant day into the answer."

LOST IN AMBIGUITY

This second group of survivors gets lost in ambiguity to move away from some hyperarousal or perceived threat. They take up residency in abstract considerations. The neuropsychologist Peter Levine points out that this shift into abstraction is called dissociation. "Dissociation is one of the most classic and subtle symptoms of trauma," he writes. "It is also one of the most mysterious. The mechanism through which it occurs is less easily explained than the experience of it or the role it plays. In trauma, dissociation seems to be a favored means of enabling a person to endure experiences that are at the moment beyond endurance—like being attacked by a lion, a rapist, an oncoming car, or a surgeon's knife. Dissociation interrupts the continuity of the felt sense."

Levine's notion of the "felt sense" can be understood as an awareness of and connection to what is occurring in the body, such as internal sensations and emotions. Bodily experiences are translated into concepts, distancing the individual from what is happening in the body. Curiously enough, while traumatized concrete learners claim they are only bodies, traumatized abstract learners claim they are only minds. This latter group needs to find safety while feeling their emotions and taking action that reflects what they truly love. Let's look more closely at what happens to folks lost in ambiguity:

1) Because being present in the here and now is mostly a bodily experience, they can easily miss what is occurring in the moment.

2) Meaning is a capacity to relate to the crucial elements of the human condition, which are inevitably ambiguous, coupled with the ability to express them through real action. Meaning is compromised by the loss of action.

3) When emotions are translated into thoughts, it becomes difficult to feel and identify emotional needs resulting in a diminished capacity for emotional intimacy.

4) Personal identity tends to become diffused amid the airiness of conceptual activity. There is a loss of an embodied sense of who they are, their strengths, their accomplishments, and what they truly desire.

5) Engaging in the rhythm of a relational dynamic is hindered as they are challenged to feel empathy for the other while connecting to a felt sense of what is important for them to communicate.

6) Typically, there is an impairment to the ability to connect to instinct, which offers a significant source of information. Levine suggests, "Instincts, therefore, are about movement—how to find food, shelter and a mate, as well as how to protect ourselves. These responses need no learning. They are hardwired in the service of our survival."

MAKING PEACE WITH THE BODY

Let's explore some ways that traumatized abstract learners can safely return to their bodies, relinquishing some measure of the comfort of being lost in ambiguity. It will mean learning to feel safe with both external and internal bodily experiences:

1) Aromatherapy to awaken the sensation of smell.
2) Therapeutic massage.
3) Reflexology.

4) Movement practices such as gentle yoga, tai chi, and dance.

5) Listening to music and noticing either the body's response and/or what emotions are being stimulated.

6) Expressing emotions to trusted others, even if it is simply what feels pleasant or unpleasant.

7) Creating soothing images of your body in scenes that feel nurturing, comforting, and tranquil, along with tracking the internal sensations, such as a slow rhythmic breath, an expansiveness in the chest, or a warmth in the cheeks, that follow holding such images.

8) Carrying a touchstone, which could be an actual stone, a medallion, or any object holding sentimental value, reminding you of your commitment to let go of being lost in ambiguity and found in your body.

9) Telling the story of returning your body to a trusted support system.

10) Employing some form of somatic psychotherapy.

We are meaning-makers, and aging does not bar us from creating meaning with depth. Although trauma can inhibit our capacity to make meaning, it need not be a permanent impediment. It may be that your innate predisposition to learn will create a particular relationship with ambiguity. Concrete learners who know how to take action can learn to safely relate to ambiguity, adding to the richness of what it means to live a meaningful life. Abstract learners can learn to have a felt sense of their bodies and take real action reflective of being somatically informed. Each group is asked to live these questions: What courage is life asking of me? What external and internal resources do I need to accept life's invitation?

I realized that no matter how old we are, unresolved trauma could be an issue as elders seek to create meaning. I wanted more clarity about what happens when trauma is addressed. What does an open and receptive relationship with ambiguity look like? What is going on if we are not literalizing ambiguity nor getting lost in it? My conversations with Emma typically led me to considerations like: What is a mature love? What is a mature spirituality? And what is a mature philosophy? I began to see how an open and receptive relationship with ambiguity supports further maturation for the soulful elder.

EASING INTO AMBIGUITY

"I appreciate what you've written about avoiding literalizing ambiguity or getting lost in it. These are significant considerations as we face aging and welcoming elderhood. So much of the meaning in our earlier lives was offered to us by society. We found a significant other or not, raised children, secured a job, made money, got promoted or changed jobs, and discovered how our gifts would support a fulfilling lifestyle. A soulful elder needs to know how to ease into ambiguity to remain a meaning-maker. The question, of course, is what does easing into ambiguity look like?" surmised Emma.

"Well, we know it's neither literalizing ambiguity nor getting lost in it. I see that it is important to see what an easy relationship with ambiguity looks like," I concurred.

"Okay, let's take a closer look. What happens when someone isn't literalizing ambiguity?" asked Emma, moving to the edge of her chair.

"My hunch is that literalizing means to translate or interpret an experience as meaning only one thing, and probably a very concrete meaning—a kind of literalizing. I guess there is rigidity, not allowing for multiple understandings of ambiguous concepts like love and courage. Consequently, there needs to be more acceptance and receptivity to the unknown possibilities for understanding some idea. There also needs to be more acceptance of the tension that likely ensues when facing the unknown," I added, feeling satisfied with the direction of our inquiry.

"Sure, there is acceptance of the unknown possibilities and the tension that might arise while relating to the unknown," Emma suggested.

"Why can the unknown create so much tension in us?" I wondered.

"Well, for one thing, when we're not sure how to define a concept, we're also not sure who we are in relation to that idea. We lose a sense of identity. To say, 'I'm not sure what love is' means 'I'm not sure who I am as someone who loves.' The societal mandate is that we are supposed to know who we are. It's allegedly what big people do. So, rather than be honest about being uncertain, we compensate by suggesting we know exactly what love is. That move shuts down the investigation, disallows us from learning more about things like love," Emma cautioned with an ease that suggested I was listening to someone who had integrated the words being spoken into action.

"I also think it would help to reconsider curiosity. Rather than see it simply as a declaration that we don't know something, see it as an earnest interest in discovering more."

"Right on! An old definition of the word *curiosity* is 'to care deeply.' Isn't that a hell of a lot better than 'I don't know what I'm talking about'? It's easier to care about getting whatever right than to care about all that can be discovered. An important key is to let go of the right-wrong template. Serious moral issues can always summon us back to a consideration of right and wrong, but for everything else, it's wise to let go. There's a lovely piece by Rumi. I think it goes something like this:

Out beyond ideas of wrongdoing and right-doing,
there is a field. I'll meet you there.
When the soul lies down in that grass,
the world is too full to talk about.
Ideas, language, even the phrase
each other doesn't make any sense."

"Wow, you memorized it! I'm impressed!"

"Some things are worth keeping close by. Talk of right and wrong almost always signals a lack of a supple attitude. Suppleness allows the mind to stretch beyond the familiar. However, that's also true of courage, whether you're into literalizing ambiguity or getting lost in it," explained Emma with a trustworthy modesty.

"Can you say more about the role of courage?"

"To interrupt an attachment to the familiar and what provides comfort, both those literalizing ambiguity and those getting lost in it will need courage. The literalizing group will need the courage to let go of claims to alleged certainty, suggesting that their declarations are beyond reproach. This group lives close to readiness for action, for implementing what they believe. That's their strength. Making meaning is a mixture of reflection and action, and each of us is either more comfortable with reflection or action. Those who get lost in ambiguity will need to find the courage to choose some specific action amid so many possibilities," Emma noted, her smile suggesting that she might belong to the latter group.

"I'm hearing how vital the role of courage is. Can you say more about how action contributes to the creation of meaning?"

"Well, getting lost in ambiguity is a way to avoid the risk of taking an action that declares who we are. Such a declaration calls for leaving the sanctuary of extended rumination. The action tells the world who we've decided to be in that moment and makes us vulnerable to criticism and rejection," Emma added, her eye contact increasing in intensity, leaving me with the feeling that she was someone who felt responsible for singing the praises of courage.

"I see the risk, but how does taking action contribute to making meaning?" I asked with a building curiosity.

"When we act, we leave the sanitized conditions of cogitating. The action will call in a myriad of existential conditions, which will inevitably add to our original meaning. We may see something new about ourselves after we act. For example, we have thought that some action of ours was extremely altruistic and, upon taking action, an element of self-interest is revealed. We may become open to a variety of responses from others, such as disagreement, appreciation, anger, confusion, acceptance, and rejection. Action places us in a new perspective, an additional way to view our meanings. Let me read this piece by Michael Meade," offered Emma. "'The soul requires an outer drama so that it can reveal its full imagination for life and its inner myth.'"

"I hear Meade saying that action or some 'outer drama' allows our 'inner myth' or story to be revealed and that 'its full imagination for life' as we encounter ideological and philosophical views, as well as a wide range of diverse beliefs, may stretch how we see ourselves and the world. I'm feeling more comfortable with the idea of easing into ambiguity. If it's all right with you, I want to recap what we have said," I suggested.

"Sure, go ahead," encouraged Emma.

"Okay, this is what I've got. We can ease into ambiguity when the following are present. One: Accepting the unknown. Two: Accepting ourselves as not knowing and coping with the tension that may be present. Three: Suspending right and wrong. Four: Holding our views with more suppleness. Five: Exercising enough courage to remain curious. Six: Exercising enough courage to take action."

"I think that covers it. These are the necessary conditions to create a personal philosophy," concluded Emma, nodding with obvious satisfaction.

8: AMBIGUITY AND
A MATURING PERSONAL PHILOSOPHY

> "The art of being wise
> is knowing what to overlook."
>
> *– William James*

A maturing personal philosophy is a critical component of a soulful path to elderhood. The word *philosophy* can be translated as "the love of wisdom." That leaves us with the task of attempting to clarify what wisdom is and what loving it looks like:

- **A maturing personal philosophy depends on a receptive and open relationship with ambiguity.** If philosophy is to remain a sacred endeavor, then it must be committed to confirming what truly matters. And what truly matters, like the fabrics of love, justice, truth, devotion, freedom, virtue, and compassion, is woven with the unknown.
- **Considering wisdom as a verb.** One way to think about wisdom is the act of creating stories about what truly matters. Writes Michael Meade, "Wisdom requires a sense of story, a feeling for where things are headed, a narrative intelligence for what is important and enduring and what is strictly temporary and mostly distracting."

- **Living in a wisdom story calls for courage.** I recall a daughter of mine dying after two days of life and me not having enough courage to face the loss. I remember being told that a nine-month-old child of mine would be one hundred percent disabled for life and me not having enough courage to face the challenge. I decided to leave a twenty-five-year marriage, knowing I did not know where to find the courage to deal with such a separation. I remember being a college professor deciding not to teach in a classroom and deciding to employ a new paradigm of learning, not knowing where the courage would come from to follow through with my vision. I remember creating a mentoring community for teenage boys and not knowing how to muster the courage to go somewhere I had never been before. In each of these life events, I was being asked not to over-literalize ambiguous considerations like commitment, loyalty, and responsibility, allowing myself instead to remain open to new and different perspectives born from the ambiguous. It would be more challenging to find the courage to risk some action rather than get lost in ambiguity. In the words of Henry David Thoreau, "The fact of thinking in oneself is not enough, it is about acting on this ground fertilized by the thought: 'For me, the moment has come to sow. For too long I stayed fallow.'" As I look back, whatever measure of courage I was able to muster mostly came from the care and support I received from mentors and friends. Remaining in a wisdom story mostly means not trying to do it alone.
- **Developing a maturing epistemology.** A personal philosophy must be energized by a maturing epistemology. We can say that epistemology is a story about how we go about knowing or supporting a fertile understanding of our experience. Some of this understanding will be about the mundane and the practical. However, if we are to be

meaning-makers, our attention must be brought to that which truly matters. The polarity of holding a committed position while experiencing doubt and curiosity will make our inquiries more trustworthy. The words of Rollo May, from his book *The Courage to Create*, bring this point home: "Commitment is healthiest when it is not *without* doubt but *in spite of* doubt. To believe fully and at the same moment to have doubts is not at all a contradiction: it presupposes a greater respect for truth, an awareness that truth always goes beyond anything that can be said or done at any given moment."

Rilke calls on us to "love our questions." He does not appeal to our ability to love our answers. Did he realize that the ego needs no encouragement to love its answers? What is so attractive about having answers? Having an alleged answer implies we have arrived at the end of some inquiry, entitled to the supposed bounty of truth. Nothing soothes the trembling of a psyche facing confusion and the ego's aspirations of being a knower more than the testimony to the procurement of an answer. With confusion diffused and the ego content to be a knower, stories about deserving attention and respect begin to settle in, offering temporary respite from the demands of ambiguity.

I find myself wondering why Rilke encourages us to "love our questions" rather than simply accept them. Could he have known about the seductive power of answers? If so, then acceptance would not be potent enough to compete with the allure of answers. Love would be needed to mitigate the ego's obsession with answers as the acculturation that takes place as our educational institutions fixate on answers. Here, again, we will need the courage to honor our curiosities to face a cultural mandate to produce answers.

9: UNITY CONSCIOUSNESS

"The reason why the world lacks unity, and lies broken and in heaps,
is, because man is disunited with himself."

– *Ralph Waldo Emerson*

I returned to Emma's wanting to discuss unity consciousness and its place on the soulful path to elderhood. My intuition was that unity consciousness, in some way, reflected a significant move beyond the ego's alleged dominion, which naturally fostered separation.

"I assume you've been reflecting more about the path to elderhood," Emma offered.

"Yes, I have. It's like planning for an extended European trip. I really want to understand where I'm going and how to get there," I described, eager to put together an elder map.

"Remember, you're already on the trip. You are rounding out the itinerary; what not to forget and what to include."

"I appreciate your encouragement and feel drawn to include unity consciousness. I'm not quite sure what it is, and yet, I believe it is important. At the very least, it must entail a significant ego adjustment," I added.

"I believe you're on to something. The ego relishes its capacity to differentiate, divide, compare, and contrast. We can say that without that ego agenda, it may be almost impossible to individuate and honor our essential uniqueness. We need to establish individuality before we can let go of it. However, the ego becomes embroiled in the task of not only inaugurating its uniqueness but also demonstrating worthiness. To walk the soulful path of elderhood, you must be able and willing to rein in the ego's obsessive strivings, or there will neither be unity consciousness nor elderhood," explained Emma, her tone suggesting that she was talking to someone who needed to learn to rein in his strivings.

"I often wonder what it takes to deactivate the ego's drive to prove the unprovable. It appears there's nothing that can ultimately satisfy the ego's thirst for validation," I pointed out.

"Well, you may have stumbled across a response to your question. It often takes many, many attempts at achieving, striving to impress, and waiting for some special someone to come and tell us that we are lovable. When each of these strategies ends over and over again in defeat, you may hear a whisper from the soul, letting you know that you are enough. The more you can hold that gentle voice, the more ready you are for living into unity consciousness. However, it can be more challenging if you are readily receiving admiration and regard from others. Then, the ego wants to keep the parade going and lives by the illusion that it is controlling the praise coming its way. Then, it is more difficult to hear the quiet voice within," noted Emma, holding both an invitation to hearing such a whisper and an understanding that it is no simple task, especially when the world is making wonderful offerings.

"I often hear people say that they want to 'be someone.' I'm not sure what that means, and my hunch is that it doesn't facilitate unity consciousness," I suggested.

"Yes, that is a popular saying. My guess is that it is a wish to be special. I often want to say to people, 'If you want to be special, get on with it and get it out of your system as soon as you can.' Your hunch is right; it won't support unity consciousness," agreed Emma.

THE HAZARDS OF BEING SPECIAL

In my counseling practice, I have heard endless strivings to be "special" or regrets over not being so. A soulful path to elder-hood calls for relinquishing the desire to be special. I first noticed that the vision of being special included a rejection of being ordinary. I began to wonder: How does someone become special? Does it serve us to see ourselves or be seen by others as special? What's wrong with being ordinary?

My second understanding was that special had been separated from unique. Uniqueness pertains to the incomparable nature of how a person grieves, loves, suffers, longs, holds power, and experiences victory, defeat, and desperation. It is how we own and develop our particular strengths and talents. Our uniqueness lives comfortably with our ordinariness as depicted by our vulnerability, hunger, need for comfort and acceptance, and our inevitable experiences of failure, loss, illness, and death. In the depth of our ordinariness, we find our place in the human community.

However, the more special we decide we are, the more we delude ourselves into believing we can outdistance our ordinariness. If an achievement possesses some unusual lofty status such as that acquired by some entertainers, Hollywood stars, professional athletes, and successful entrepreneurs, then such folks run the risk of believing that their specialness makes them impervious to ordinary frailties. Such distortion makes those people exceedingly vulnerable.

The third and most unfortunate take was the belief that becoming special somehow makes us deserving of love. I was beginning to understand the striving and the pain involved with attaining some special status. It may be worthwhile to look at some of the distinguishing features between special, unique, and ordinary and the implications of these differences:

- We may have liberated ourselves from King George III in 1776, but we never lost our love affair with hierarchy. The status of being special relies upon hierarchy: "Somebody is up, and somebody is down." Acknowledging uniqueness is not exempt from comparing lifestyles but doesn't do it within a hierarchal framework. We can simultaneously appreciate the uniqueness of others as accentuating the distinctive features of our characters.

- Special means attempting to transcend the more disagreeable aspects of the human condition, such as envy, lethargy, fear, desperation, confusion, self-loathing, and defeat. While unique and ordinary welcome a fuller picture of our character, we should be willing to appreciate the not-so-celebrated qualities as a more honest depiction of humanity.

- Special is typically laced with strong threads of perfectionism, preventing us from truly appreciating who we are now. On the other hand, "unique and ordinary" is expressed by acceptance, allowing us to settle into ourselves with less of the angst of striving.

- Special typically relies upon external standards for verification, placing a great deal of power outside of ourselves, while unique and ordinary are confirmed by living a self-examined life, leaving the power to substantiate our uniqueness with us. I recently worked with a mother who wanted to be a "special" mom, driven by perfectionism, which placed the confirmation of her specialness in the hands of her ten-year-old son, who appeared to know exactly what to do with the offering. "My son seems to be unusually demanding, while I find myself feeling increasingly inadequate as a parent," explained the mom. "He may be aware that he has control of how you're going to feel about yourself as a parent, and he's cashing in," I suggested. "Are you saying that he somehow knows I am invested in his approval?" she asked. I replied, "Yes, I am. Try defining yourself as a wonderfully unique and ordinary mom, and see what happens." Several weeks later, she reported that harmony had returned to the home.

- Special runs the risk of getting caught in endless undertakings of attempting to be impressive at the sacrifice of authenticity; "unique and ordinary" remains devoted to increased expressions of being genuine.

- Special can easily become obsessed with achieving for the sake of attaining a lofty status. Such laboring can also suggest that achievements have become temporary inoculations against the infection of self-loathing. Meanwhile, "unique and ordinary" experiences achieving as an opportunity to grow, learn, and serve.

- Special by being hierarchal tends to separate us from others. In our comparisons, we either elevate others, leaving us prone to envy and jealousy, or we diminish ourselves for not being special enough. "Unique and ordinary" unites us with others as we hold our distinctive features within the framework of our common humanity.

- Special tends to breed arrogance and hubris. Failed attempts at achieving some special status can easily move us into an inflationary pattern. That is, if we don't feel special, we can generate an inflated persona, pretending to be special, which is also known as arrogance.

It is impossible to avoid getting caught up by the seductions of "special" as our society bombards us with infusions of the importance of hierarchy: the best, the biggest, the loudest, the strongest, the winningest, the smartest, and the fastest. We do well to remember the role of the horseman assigned to approach a Roman general riding into Rome following a victorious campaign, whispering, "Glory is but fleeting." And so, it is with "special," allegedly attained by some promotion, recognition, or achievement—"Special is but fleeting"—unlike our experiences of "unique and ordinary," which are enduring and sustainable.

"Unique and ordinary" can be endlessly understood in new ways, welcomed, appreciated, and developed. However, it may be important to allow our most fervent attempts to be special to run their course until we either discover that even when temporarily attaining some special status, we have merely postponed the responsibility to create and sustain genuine self-love. It may be that from that perspective, we can see ourselves in others, the best and worst of us, as unity consciousness becomes more palpable.

BACK AT EMMA'S

"The writing I've been doing on the attachment to being special has brought me to a deeper place regarding getting honest with myself about my obsession with being special along the way," I offered with more than a hint of embarrassment as I looked away, suggesting I had just shared a secret.

"It's not all that easy to admit, is it? And yet, it reflects the very core of being human. We want to believe that we can secure some way of being entitled to be loved. All of our strategies circumvent being genuine, which is the only way to set the stage for at least the possibility of being loved. Once you can be gentle with your quest for being special, you will likely find more compassion for those on the special journey, as well as those pretending to be special, realizing how far they have stepped away from themselves," explained Emma, her offering feeling quite large, like a guide to life, and yet with a tone sounding so matter of fact.

"That sure sounds like the business of soulful elderhood. The compassion you speak of is a significant act of emotional generosity."

"You're right. It's extremely generous, and that level of generosity comes more easily when we view what people are doing through the lens of love. Then, we see others seeking love, forgetting that they deserve love, being impressive enough to be entitled to being loved, forgetting how to love themselves and engaging in some activity that they mistakenly believe has nothing to do with love," concluded Emma, sounding as if she were simply giving me directions to the local supermarket.

Sometimes, when Emma spoke, I felt like my brain and every other vital system in my being slowed way down, as if not to move in fear of distracting from the measure of truth I was present for. This was one of those moments. It was asking for stillness. Yes, asking me to learn how to remain in the presence of truth in the hope of reducing the seduction to augment, explain, and demonstrate. Later, I would look back on these moments as the antidote to my propensity for delusion.

I left Emma's that day thankful for all that I had received. What she gave me became compost for my curiosity as I began to wonder how unity consciousness can be supported once the ego relaxes a bit. However, I remember Emma quoting a college professor by the name of Jordon Peterson, regarding hierarchy. I did some research and found the following in his book, *12 Rules for Life*: "We (the *sovereign we*, the *we* that has been around since the beginning of life) have lived in a dominance hierarchy for a long, long time. We were struggling for position before we had skin, or hands, or lungs, or bones. There is little more natural than culture. Dominance hierarchies are older than trees."

HIERARCHY VS. HOLDING RANK

I had a strong critical reaction to Peterson's claim that living in a hierarchal structure is extremely natural. I soon realized that my reaction was much about feeling the hopelessness of unity consciousness if Peterson's position had any credibility. I eventually settled down, realizing that hierarchy and unity consciousness may not be an unmanageable polarity. It meant remaining curious about what might make the existence of hierarchy so natural.

One position advocated by Peterson and others is how neurochemistry impacts behavior. The thinking is that when we are in positions of comfort, safety, and satisfaction, we are riding on pleasant feelings generated by serotonin. To be one up, holding a significant amount of privilege with an entitlement regarding getting our needs met, gives us a dose of serotonin. That serotonin hit reinforces certain behaviors related to the benefits of being positioned on top.

We can use the image of herd animals maneuvering for safety by pushing toward the middle of the pack, thus avoiding the margins where one is more susceptible to predators. The herd metaphor suggests that being marginalized socially lends itself to feeling more insecure and vulnerable, as well as experiencing more doses of cortisol than serotonin.

Certainly, hierarchal structures are self-perpetuated and maintained by those belonging to certain families, organizations, clubs, schools, and fraternities. Privilege and entitlement are passed on to subsequent generations of members. Also, those who possess certain talents and skills can easily rise to the surface when their competencies are needed or desired. An example might be what happens to the status of physicians when we desire health, to clergy when we desire eternal life, to teachers when we want an education, or to janitors when we desire a clean and safe apartment building. We are constantly creating hierarchies based on our needs.

There are numerous ways in which hierarchy gets established, but they all point to a key question: How do we have hierarchy serve all rather than simply meet the immediate gratification of those whose gifts are acknowledged? How can the service of hierarchy reflect some measure of unity consciousness? The service of hierarchy can be easily haunted by our experiences. We learn in schools, playgrounds, and clubs that some kids are acknowledged, and some are not. To be a kid whose gifts are not acknowledged may lead us to believe there is something wrong with us. These early childhood experiences may be where the perils of classicism are bred, turning either against ourselves or against those riding high.

I recall an experience I had as a doctoral student while studying leadership with Ken Blanchard, who at that time was considered to be a leading authority on the topic. My classmates had left the room to break for lunch while I remained to write some additional notes. Professor Blanchard was gathering his belongings at the front of the room when a janitor entered, disposing of trash and putting tables and chairs into order. Professor Blanchard turned to the janitor and thanked him for the attention he brought to the needs of the room. I heard the genuineness of Professor Blanchard's gratitude as he acknowledged the janitor for bringing beauty and order to the teaching environment. The scene has remained with me throughout the years as I am reminded that even as a world-renowned author and teacher, a reach beyond one's hierarchal status with an appreciation for those who serve and support my purpose can happen.

THE CONSEQUENCES OF HIERARCHY REMAINING UNCONSCIOUS

- When serotonin alone drives hierarchy, it tends to make some groups separate and special.
- It can suggest that those whose gifts are acknowledged are superior and those whose gifts aren't acknowledged are inferior.

- It can restrict privilege and entitlement to only people whose gifts are acknowledged.
- It creates alienation and ignorance between those whose gifts are acknowledged and those whose aren't.
- It breeds resentment and distrust between the two groups.
- Holders of acknowledged gifts lose the capacity to self-generate personal worth as they depend on contrasting themselves to holders of unacknowledged gifts for an injection of feeling positive about themselves.
- There can be serious confusion about how the two sets of gifts are interdependent.
- The resentment of those with unacknowledged gifts easily morphs into a need for revenge.

HOLDING RANK

Holding rank can be an effective tool for supporting the polarity between hierarchy and unity consciousness:

- It is meant to identify and employ the unique gifts of individuals for the benefit of the collective. It assumes that everyone is gifted and that some gifts may receive more notoriety and appreciation depending on the prevailing needs.
- Those possessing certain valued gifts are not ascribed superiority but, rather, greater responsibility.
- Those possessing certain gifts are encouraged to be in the service of others.
- Identifying rank with particular gifts allows us to know where needed resources exist.
- Holding hierarchy mindfully means being aware that hierarchy is contextual, addressing the needs and desires of a person or system and who possesses the competencies to meet those needs.

THE CORNERSTONE OF ELDERING

The danger of an aging ego is the tendency to see ourselves as having arrived. The arrival is often referenced as having achieved something resembling wisdom or, perhaps, deserving of respect. An old definition of the word *respect* is "looking back at" or "regarding." I would suggest that we all deserve respect, being regarded and not ignored.

Soulful eldering is not interested in arriving but rather in being devoted to serving something larger than oneself. Let the serotonin flow freely when an elder devotes themself to bringing more sustainability to a community, an organization, or a young person! Rather than expect respect from others, elders can give witness to others. There are so many who have no experience of being seen by a father. See them, see their gifts, see their dreams, see their challenges, and see their longing to be seen.

There will be disbelievers, those whose fathers never saw them. They don't dare imagine another way. They will be convinced that you only want to demonstrate the prowess of your insights and skills, of you dismissing a younger individual's desire to be regarded. Be mindful of what is beyond your control, trusting that younger people are waiting for you.

What we offer as elders is not mostly altruistic. We give because we are in the winter of our lives, and we've come to know the deep joy of our offerings. There simply is not a great deal of time left for giving to take place, and we heartfully know now that is the promise our souls carry. We may hold rank due to our life experience and mastery over some trade or field of study. The polarity of hierarchy and unity consciousness loses its tension when held in devotion to serving. That devotional spirit accompanied by a measure of discernment will reveal where our final years need to be lived. We come to understand where we belong in the winter of our lives. Such belonging brings more suppleness to the polarity of hierarchy and unity consciousness.

IMAGINATION

My reflections continued to bring me to the role of imagination. I realized how much I had taken my understanding of imagination for granted. I began by considering what some ancient definitions of the word might be. I found an old meaning of the word *imagination*: "to form an image of, to picture in one's mind." I decided that when I'm imagining, I'm creating a picture in my mind of something different or more than what I typically experience through touch, sound, or sight. Then, I came across a quote by Charles Dickens that I wanted to share with Emma.

"I've been thinking about what can happen once the ego eases up with its determination to differentiate and separate. My hunch is that it can be helpful to allow ourselves to be informed by our imagination, creating new a new image based on unity rather than some hierarchal matrix of who's acknowledged and who's not," I concluded, feeling comfortable with the direction of my considerations.

"Yes, it's a big shift, moving from separation to unity. Most aging folks won't do it. They will continue to employ the old hierarchal lens now, as inherent losses move from those with acknowledged gifts to those with gifts that are unacknowledged. It's a sad thing. Tell me more about the role of imagination in supporting unity consciousness," Emma encouraged.

"Well, I'm thinking it's about creating a new picture or image in our minds, one that unites us with nature and other people. However, I am wondering: What is the creative material that gives rise to the new picture and allows the image to be embodied or fully alive?"

"As the ego settles, moderating its belief in the preeminent nature of the intellect, you can allow yourself to be more informed by your heart. Differentiating, categorizing, separating, and analyzing are mitigated by compassion, sympathy, and empathy. However, the most powerful creative material supporting unity consciousness is allowing yourself to be touched and moved. The key is to permit deep sentiment to inform. It will take courage as the ego pipes up, exercising its best efforts to minimize sentiment in favor of intellectual pursuits," concluded Emma.

"That's true. Why is a deep sentiment so much more difficult to trust than an intellectual musing?"

"There was no place in your education where deep sentiment was asked for, encouraged, and prized. It is also more ambiguous, often leading to more questions. Of course, sentiment is the cradle of curiosity, and that may be its greatest gift. Essentially, it is allowing for the heart to have a voice, and the heart is essential to the soulful path to elderhood and unity consciousness," noted Emma.

"I'm noticing that I am touched and moved more and, sometimes, I feel embarrassed. You know, I see a simple act of affection or kindness and think, 'I'm kind of losing it,'" I said, sensing how much I had minimized being informed by my heart, diminishing it as frivolous, sentimental, and empty.

"Yes, that kind of embarrassment comes from living too long in the house of the ego. Luckily, interesting ideas begin to fall short of receiving the ego's endorsement. It's time to move in with the soul," beamed Emma, reassuring me that she now was where I was hoping to go.

"I'm thinking that the new picture we create in our minds needs to be trustworthy on some level. I came across this quote by Charles Dickens that suggests what makes imagining trustworthy. He said, 'My imagination would never have served me as it has, but for the habit of commonplace, humble, patient, daily toiling, drudging attention.' What do you think?"

"I like it. I think he's saying that before you get into imagining what's possible, let yourself be with what is here and now. It's damn good advice. When you don't know how to make peace with reality, there can be a strong seduction into the dream world of imagining, where reality is sanitized. When this happens, you sacrifice a resiliency created by daily toiling and drudging attention, a resiliency that is also capable of manifesting the dream or the new picture being imagined," Emma added, both of us knowing that truth had joined us.

"I hear you suggesting that a devoted relationship with 'what is' can elicit a relationship with 'what can be.' I see a shadow element of mine here. Rather than be curious about what a situation is truly asking for, I tend to quickly go to what would make it better," I confessed, sensing my attitude that if I can make it better, then I make myself better.

"That's a great catch. You want what is and what could be to be in a relationship. The key is not to charge imagination with the task of canceling what is but rather to have it simply be an ambassador of change," Emma concluded.

"It sounds like imagination and acceptance need to be in a relationship," I offered.

"Yes, acceptance is the beginning place. How would you define acceptance?" asked Emma.

"Well, acceptance is ... I know what it is; I'm just not sure what to say," I added, feeling embarrassed and realizing I got embarrassed quite often around Emma without her ever intentionally provoking it.

"An old definition of the word *acceptance* is 'to receive willingly.' It may be worthwhile to explore what might get in the way of receiving willingly and what it might take to get there," Emma explained.

I took Emma's advice and began wondering about acceptance.

ACCEPTANCE

Is what flows in the name of acceptance ever pure? Maybe acceptance is a welcoming. At its best, we receive someone or something into our neighborhoods, homes, bodies, minds, and hearts. Uncle Fred arrives for Thanksgiving dinner, and our welcome is mitigated by the expectation that he will be obnoxious, drink too much, and offer a long itinerary of his upcoming achievements. Life is constantly presenting us with the opportunity to decide whether we should deepen our capacity to accept what's coming at us or exercise our wills, enacting some form of change.

The will is either like a warm spring breeze, softening and calming what it touches, or an arctic blast, jolting everything in its way. Our challenge is to continue to craft the kind of discernment that tells us how much will to put forward. When life acts in direct contrast to what we want, a tension occurs that will typically have our wills recoiling at some unwanted piece of life. It could be something said or something done that rubs us wrong. The ego is convinced it knows better and may be able to summon some tolerance at best.

Pride quickly joins forces with the will, helping it feel good about itself. Pride then proceeds to offer arguments demonstrating why and how life went astray. The prideful will stands strong, indignant about life forgetting its mandate to serve my revered life: How could life forget its purpose?

As waves of defeat crash over our wills, again and again, eroding the thinking that life is in our employ, we may gradually come to notice—and accept—that life does not appear to be in the business of serving our lives. Yet, there may be a place for our will to participate, to live out some desire. It may take a while for the dizziness to subside as we gain some understanding of how small that place may be. Life does appear to want our participation rather than us contracting into depression and cynicism because we have become so disillusioned about the reduced size of our participation. Life welcomes our joining. We can notice small expressions of life's invitation when we are acknowledged, seen, and appreciated by others.

"God grant me the serenity to accept the things I cannot change, the courage to change the things that I can, and the wisdom to know the difference." This simple prayer reminds us about how to renew our relationships with life. The request for "serenity" comes about as we hold our hopes for life's cooperation with more suppleness. We gradually shift away from the view that life is either helping or not helping us. Such a shift suggests the ego is willing to reconcile with life's inevitable dominance. In that reconciliation, tolerance morphs into welcome.

It doesn't mean we always like how life impacts us. The ego may need time to lick its wounds, gradually returning to accessing enough courage to attend to what is in its control. The wisdom needed to distinguish what is in and out of our control deepens as we protest less about life's challenges and losses. Curiosity replaces protest and yields more clarity about what we can control. However, the appropriateness of acting courageously may not yield the immediate satisfaction that complaining does.

Wisdom about what is in and out of our control has a double edge. On the one hand, it allows us to let go of fruitless efforts to impact people and situations in which we are powerless. On the other hand, we are left with the task of attending to our own lives and finding the courage to ask the questions that matter: What am I being asked to learn? What do I need to let go of? What is difficult for me to admit? Where do I come from? Where am I going? Who is coming with me? What do I love? To whom or what am I devoted? What are my gifts? What are my wounds? What healing is my life asking for? How effective am I at allowing love in? How can I best serve?

Allowing ourselves to be increasingly guided by the serenity prayer happens when we decide we are here to serve life and not for life to serve us. An old definition of the word *serve* is "to meet the needs of." As elders, we can move our lives to a new level by being guided by the question "What is life needing from me?" This question greatly helps the ego to find its rightful place and surrender claims to supremacy. Also, "What is life needing from me?" is different from "What is my life needing from me?" The former question is somewhat more ego-reducing.

There are endless ways to respond to the question "What does life need from me?" I've come to believe that I typically do not need to ponder the question endlessly. Life has a way of getting my attention when it comes to what it needs, especially when it needs my acceptance.

Several years ago, feeling responsible for preparing dinner for my family, I decided to forge forward with my three-year-old daughter, Sarah, to the grocery store. Being accompanied by Sarah during such an outing was no simple task. Due to her rare neurological disorder, it could be quite challenging to navigate the aisles of a grocery store without her grabbing items off of shelves and aggressively grasping at passing customers.

I arrived at the checkout counter somewhat relieved, as no one had been accosted and cereal boxes remained in their proper positions. The trick now was to get to the front of the shopping cart to unload groceries onto the conveyer built quickly, since it meant leaving Sarah unattended, sitting in the seat of the cart. I was convinced that I was quickly moving toward success as I hurled groceries onto the counter, the checkout girl looking somewhat worried about the possibility of a can of tuna making its way in her direction.

Just then, I looked up to see Sarah with one of her vice-like grips on the arm of an elderly woman. I pushed my way vigorously to the seat of the cart, readying myself for the task of dislodging Sarah's hand from the woman's arm without injuring either of them.

The woman quickly stopped me and yelled, "No, don't; no one has touched me in over twenty-five years!"

I quickly paused, overwhelmed by her declaration and noticing that the six patrons standing in line behind us were paused in a heavy silence. The cashier was motionless. It was as if we had all been transported out of the ordinary reality of a grocery store to something demanding our attention and reverence. I have no idea how much time had passed when Sarah gently let go of the arm of her own accord.

As we left the store, I felt that there was so much for me to accept. Sarah's disability was not simply unfortunate but, obviously, also a gift. I was being asked to accept that Sarah's presence in the store was not simply something for me to dread. There was also the acceptance of the elderly woman's entitlement to have her needs met, as well as the acceptance that the exchange between her and Sarah would temporarily prohibit the checkout process for anyone waiting in our line. There was also the acceptance of how much mystery can accompany a visit to the grocery store. I began to understand how much acceptance can give birth to deeper levels of unity consciousness.

ACCEPTANCE AND DISCERNMENT

I was curious whether Emma had anything else to say about acceptance.

"I've been doing some reflection on acceptance, and I'm wondering what you might add," I requested.

"I read what you sent to me, and I like the idea of

acceptance as a welcome. It can be challenging for the ego to welcome what it doesn't understand, and it's not comfortable with what lives directly behind the will. It knows that what takes up residency behind the will is likely to be out of its control. And, of course, the role of discernment is critical. That is, we must decide whether we are issuing too much acceptance or not enough," added Emma.

"The idea that someone is feeling or offering too much acceptance isn't addressed much. It seems that if you can get a great deal of acceptance going, then that is certainly the mark of a good person," I replied.

"Yes, we tend to praise highly accepting people, mostly because we can count on them to treat us well and not get contentious. However, issuing too much acceptance typically is about covert deal-making: 'Don't forget how much acceptance I offered you and don't give me any trouble in the future,'" Emma pointed out.

"I get that. Is there any other reason that too much acceptance is a problem?"

"Yes, not only is it about non-verbal deals; it can also be about the suspension of authenticity and the enabling of someone's disempowerment," cautioned Emma.

"What exactly is inauthentic about someone's excessive acceptance?"

"Well, for one, the person doesn't experience as much acceptance as is being offered. Second, they are likely eliminating some level of disapproval, annoyance, and/or unacceptance. This suggests that they are not being genuinely positioned, especially when it pertains to unacceptable behavior. I'm sure you've heard it said: 'The worst thing a good person can do in the presence of evil is to be quiet,'" Emma explained.

"How can I hone my discernment so that I'm clear about seeing injustice, oppression, or even evil?" I asked.

"That's a great question. It is critical to know how to refine your discernment, to not be easily caught in a distortion or eager to make someone out to be wrong because you feel uncomfortable. Fine-tuning your discernment is mostly an inside job. Let your projections and criticisms of others reflect what you are denying about yourself. It may be your insensitivity, your arrogance, your impatience, your self-righteousness, or your self-pity. Be curious about what these darker elements of your character are asking for. Finally, commit to forgiving yourself and generating a larger acceptance of your humanity. Let yourself engage in a regular inventory, where you ask whether you made choices taking you away from your core values, where you have honored what you believe and what you feel grateful for. If you discover that you engaged in some action that violated a core value, let yourself feel shame or guilt. Although these are certainly darker energies, your values are allegedly what you are committed to honoring. Therefore, to violate them distances you from the light of what you cherish. Hopefully, you will not slip into the depths of self-pity, remembering that your highest responsibility is to make your way back to self-forgiveness," asserted Emma.

"I see what you're saying. I'm just not clear about how I move from my darker qualities and violating my values to generating a clear and discerning position about the behavior of others," I admitted.

"Practice, practice, and more practice. You choose to be alive, you choose to take risks, and you choose to continue to fumble toward enlightenment. Due to your fumbling, you hurt others, you hurt yourself, and you allow yourself to be seduced away from your values, sacrificing your integrity for some ego-infested escapade, which allegedly will bring you something that cannot be humanly acquired. You stumble your way into a refined discernment, and from that lens, you can see what hurts others, what obstructs their growth, what eats at their self-care, and what will not sustain a genuine love of life," Emma shared, the truth of her words palpable in the room.

A BLESSING FOR UNITY CONSCIOUSNESS

Come to know how much categorizing, dividing,
differentiating, and separating you need to do.
Certainly, honoring your uniqueness is an honorable task.
The "I" you uphold is the beginning place,
the place from which you can choose to unite.

Comparing and contrasting happens in the house of the ego.
How many times will you need to find yourself
either at the top or the bottom of the heap?
Let yourself come to know how fleeting that top place is.
It's like a warm Spring breeze offering a tender embrace,
and before you know it, it moves on, never to be possessed.

The ego exercises heavy lifting, scrambling toward the top.
And then, one day, drained by these strivings,
your gaze drifts downward, knowing you depend on
that alleged bottom dweller to make sense of your climb.
Trust your fatigue, listening to the encouragement to let go.
Notice what comes as you release unnecessary toil.

Now, more comfortable with so much less to prove,
you find yourself drifting down toward your heart,
no longer tethered to unnecessary strivings.
You come to know greater unity with your own heart.
You are touched and moved;
numbness is no longer a way to live.
Your heart is no longer a stranger.

What you see and hear is given permission to enter you.
You are pierced by it.

You are touched and reminded that you were
never really alone and separate.
You were simply searching for yourself.
Now, looking toward yourself
is so much less tied to being special.
Such a wish even feels silly and so easy to release.

You see yourself in places that were off-limits.
You see yourself in the man bragging,
the person shying away from some risk,
the one who is lost,
and the guy breaking down Capitol doors
who's desperately afraid of being forgotten
as he watches women come into power
and a population become browner by the day.

Generosity comes easy now.
It's not meant to prove anything,
and it never implies that something is lost.
You come to know giving as receiving.
You're older now, not simply in years;
your soul finds ease in a large version of acceptance.
Peace embraces you now,
and you bow in thanks for all you have been given.

10: LETTING GO OF A BORROWED ETHOS

"The only meaningful life is a life that strives for the individual
realization—absolute and unconditional—of its own particular law.
To the extent that a man is untrue to the law of his being, he has
failed to realize his own life's meaning."

– Carl Jung

"I'm noticing a level of bodily peace as I live with more unity consciousness. I guess that I'm efforting less to prove, demonstrate, and establish my uniqueness. I like it," I shared, realizing I was speaking to someone who had been walking a soulful path to elderhood. This reminder left me feeling deeply accompanied.

"Yes, unity consciousness offers the ego an opportunity to relax. You have already expressed your distinguishing features as a particular wave in a large ocean. Now, it's time to settle back and appreciate the majesty of the ocean you belong to. You gradually will become less troubled by the polarity of separate and united," explained Emma.

"I know that what you're saying about the separate and united polarity is important for me to understand. Can you say more about it?" I implored.

"Sure, I can say more. But, as much as understanding this polarity, you'll need to learn to live it," added Emma.

"How do I live the polarity?"

"Well, you certainly will need to let go of a borrowed ethos," Emma pointed out, leaning forward, suggesting I should take in what she was offering.

"Yeah, this sounds important. However, I'm not sure what an ethos is, never mind a borrowed one," I admitted with more than a hint of embarrassment.

"Not a problem. An ethos is comprised of the values, the beliefs, what you cherish and are devoted to, and even what you worship; all contribute to your spirit. The hitch, of course, is we go through life borrowing bits and pieces of ethos belonging to others," Emma explained, and as she did, I knew I was hearing what I needed to hear.

"I want to hear more about why we borrow stuff that seems so important to who we are. Why not simply go with what's important to us?" I wondered.

"That takes courage. We emerge from the womb with a deep DNA-knowing that our survival is greatly determined by our affiliation with the tribe. We're afraid of being alone, so we get on with the business of living a borrowed ethos. We buy into the illusion that we can unite before we separate. Instead, the wave returns to the ocean only after it boldly and uniquely crashes upon the shore," concluded Emma.

"I think you're saying that there's a way in which, if I take my personal ethos seriously, I will gradually come to find the spirit of the human condition. And that is how the polarity of separate and united can be held," I offered in the hope that I was not too far off from what Emma intended to convey.

"I believe Carl Jung claimed that if we go down deep enough into our souls, we eventually discover the soul of humanity. It calls for elders to be willing to go that far down into their own souls, which calls for a measure of courage. It means being willing to stay with the mystery of the soul, allowing the descent to reveal its offerings," explained Emma.

"Is there a way you would recommend doing that?"

"Oh, there are many ways. The path I'm partial to is offered by the poet Rainer Maria Rilke and what he says about living questions in his 'Letters to a Young Poet,'" recommended Emma.

LIVING THE QUESTIONS

"I would like to beg you, dear Sir, as well as I can, to have patience with everything unresolved in your heart and to try to love the questions themselves as if they were locked rooms or books written in a very foreign language. Don't search for the answers, which could not be given to you now, because you would not be able to live them. And the point is to live everything. Live the questions now. Perhaps then, someday in the future, you will gradually, without even noticing it, live your way into the answer."

I took Emma's advice and began reflecting on the above passage by Rilke. I certainly enjoyed and appreciated my time with Emma, and now she was more of a muse for me. I could hear her curiosity resonating with Rilke's quote.

I began wondering about Rilke's advice to "be patient with everything unresolved in the heart." The more I stayed with the passage, the greater faith I had that more would be revealed regarding a soulful path to elderhood. I was curious about a typical reaction to what was unresolved in my heart.

For one, "unresolved" might suggest I don't know what I'm talking about. The lure of answers is that they can be an alleged testimony of knowledge. Unresolved might imply I don't know what to do, that I'm unable to act decisively, which surely is not complementary to my manhood. Also, "unresolved" suggests I'm without direction. I get it. "Unresolved" places my ego on notice. Being patient with what is unresolved in my heart means being able to push through the shame of not having an answer, not being able to act boldly or have a direction.

After encouraging patience with what is unresolved, Rilke recommends loving the questions. Foremost, Rilke offers an alternative to feeling shame because we don't have enough answers. Second, loving the questions seems to imply a faith that they are pointing us in an important direction, especially if they are referring to concerns that truly matter, like love, devotion, freedom, creativity, integrity, and morality. Third, the questions honor the depth and breadth of these important considerations, which are emblematic of soulful elderhood. Fourth, loving the questions calls for a renewal of humility by which we accept that the inquiry is much bigger than us.

I began to feel very curious about what it would take to focus on loving the questions. I also began to wonder what might happen if I wasn't patient with what was unresolved in my heart. Well, I certainly would run the risk of adopting what James Hollis calls "contrived certainty," which is a weak scaffolding for generating a worldview. Second, I could easily succumb to taking on a borrowed ethos, living my life through someone else's values and beliefs. Third, anything unresolved in my heart would not likely be some trivial matter, but again, topics deserving attention and honoring, truly emblematic of a soulful elderhood, which would not happen by hastily grabbing for some answer.

I found my ego resisting the idea that answers might not be given to me now because I might not be ready to live them. Anyway, what does it mean to be ready to live an answer? It took a while for me to get beyond my complaining ego and the voice of pride insisting that, at my age, I'm prepared to live whatever sound answer comes my way. I was given pause when I allowed for an answer to the question "What does it mean to live an answer?"

I decided that a genuine answer is something we love and

allow to guide us, letting it give rise to real choices. Otherwise, we're not living the answer but simply entertaining it as a guest. I began to see that in being patient with our questions and loving them, we allow them to become the compost for growing answers that come to maturity. Suddenly, the idea of answers belonging to me seemed silly. They were given to me.

Rilke's claim that "you will gradually, without even noticing it, live your way into the answer" began to sit with me more comfortably. My hunch was that he was saying something similar to Emma's remarks about discernment. Answers are not calling for more rumination but rather for a more lived life. Similar to Rilke's suggestion to "live everything," Nietzsche said, *"Amor fati,"* or "Love fate." The willingness to risk, to fumble, to get hurt and disillusioned, be defeated, or get lost in triumph—all provide both the answers we seek as well as the possible maturity it will take to live them.

I began to see that the hallmark of a soulful elder is to love an answer by being willing to let go of it, as a parent would with a maturing child. Not necessarily discarding it, but rather allowing it to give rise to more questions driven by a curiosity about what truly matters, appreciating that those concerns cannot be exhausted by any number of inquiries. There is an inherent bowing to the immensity of the journey to which the soulful elder feels deeply privileged to walk.

LIVING INTIMATELY

"I'm starting to think that the Initiation into soulful elderhood will likely continue until I die," I offered with a note of dismay, hoping I could get it done before I ran out of years.

"I think that I hear your attachment to arriving. What would arriving look like?" asked Emma with an inquisitive gaze that possessed a subtle note of condescension.

"Oh, I don't know. Maybe taking a break, getting some measure of respite," I offered, hoping she would not view me as a slacker.

"I like what you're insinuating. The soulful path to elderhood relinquishes excessive striving and urgency. We've talked about the importance of the moment. See if you can see it as the place to arrive. Let go of the idea of arriving at some future destination. Then, you can imagine the moment as holding you," Emma explained, her shoulders dropping and her body appearing to be embraced by the chair she sat in as if she were demonstrating how to relax into life.

"I'm not sure what it means to let the moment hold me," I admitted, very curious about Emma's explanation.

"You greet the moment with your breath. As you inhale or inspire, you receive the air the moment has prepared for you. That's how living intimately begins. You receive life's offering of breath. As in all intimate encounters, don't leave abruptly. Let yourself tarry there, your shoulders dropping, fists opening, and jaw releasing. See how it is to open to the moment's gift of spaciousness. The moment makes room for what you bring to it. Release your laboring and receive the moment's welcome," encouraged Emma, her words sounding foreign yet all too familiar.

"I'm not sure what 'releasing laboring' looks like," I said, feeling a bit less restrained about needing more information.

"I get it. It is tough to get a keen sense of what lies at your core. You simply live too close to it. We can make this about your professional life or simply the demands you place upon yourself along the way. However, anyone with a large heart begins excessively laboring very early in life. You can give it up now and learn to live more intimately," offered Emma, seemingly suggesting that I may be one of those who lived with a large heart. In any case, I wanted to be.

"Is this one of those 'if I want to step into the future calling, such as eldering, then I need to look to the past moments?" I asked, sounding more like a statement than a question.

"Sure, you've done enough work on yourself to know who's waiting for you back there, engaged in heavy lifting," asserted Emma, raising her right hand and index finger, pointing toward the ceiling.

"The early laboring was wanting to save my mother. I knew how much shame she carried and how scared she was of life. I guess saving her would have meant helping her love herself, helping her let go of shame, and assisting her to see life as a gift rather than some nemesis," I admitted with a quiet note of appreciation for the son in me who loved.

"And your father?"

"Well, he was terrified of living his gifts, risking being who he was meant to be. I wish I could have helped him see what he had to offer the world and to go and make the offering!" I exclaimed with more volume and energy than I had antici-pated and then quietly sobbed, welcoming Emma's ac-ceptance.

"You loved them, and it was very hard to watch them suf-fer. However, you cannot embrace the elderhood waiting for you while either chastising yourself for not being able to save them or being up to the business of compensating by trying to save others. This is all excessive laboring. At this point in your life, do what you love as much as possible. The moment re-joices in offering you the space and opportunity to live your love. Do it for your children, your grandchildren, and your an-cestors," Emma encouraged with a puff of breath escaping from her lips and in a tone that left me feeling liberated.

"It sounds like the task of eldering is really saving myself," I offered, feeling a bit dubious about such an endeavor.

"Of course, that's the beginning of a mature spirituality, and there's nothing more characteristic of someone on a soul-ful path of elderhood," Emma insisted, her eyebrows turning up with a slight nod, suggesting some reinforcement of her position.

"Saving myself and a mature spirituality. Let's talk more about that," I continued, eager to hear Emma's take.

"I suggest you spend some time with the topic, and we can explore more together later," Emma returned, once again inviting me back into myself.

11: A MATURE SPIRITUALITY

"A mature spirituality asks me to grow up. Growing up, at least,
means that we accept full responsibility for our lives. We are,
all of us, still responsible for meeting our needs, not some magical
other, someone who will fix it for us, explain what it all means, in-
struct us in what we are supposed to do, and if we are lucky,
take care of us so we don't have to grow up after all."

– James Hollis

It is challenging to do anything mature when a mystery is involved. The dilemma is that so much is woven with mystery,
such as love, intimacy, truth, virtue, courage, and God. During
couple-counseling sessions, one partner may turn to the other
and say, "Just tell me what to do and I'll do it!" Often said by
the male, such words excessively literalize and infantilize love
and emotional intimacy to mean, "I just need my mom to tell
me what to do." Such a dynamic condemns the couple to an
immature marriage.

Similar dynamics happen between teachers and students
when bright-eyed students sit in the front row, prepared to
write down the teacher's every word. The plan is to feed it
back to the instructor in the hopes of achieving academic success. This educational process makes for immature students,
who, when outside of classrooms, are waiting to hear from
someone who allegedly possesses the right answers.

So, it is often in religion or on a spiritual path that participants wait for a clergy person to announce how they will be
saved or not saved. The parishioner is declaring, "I don't want
to be responsible for my soul." Quite often, the fervor driving
the parishioners as well as the clergy to some lofty virtuous
state which will offer salvation has dire consequences. The
darker creaturely traits like lust, greed, and vanity go denied
and suppressed until they reach irrepressible status and get
acted out in nefarious ways. I recall an old mentor saying to
me, "Stop trying to be so damn good; you're going to end up
doing something you'll deeply regret."

We might say that an immature spirituality takes over as
we abdicate responsibility for deciding how we are going to
live. Said responsibility can be given to any leader or some celestial being. It doesn't matter. What matters is that we don't
want to be responsible for creating a life.

Take the origin story of Adam and Eve, for example, which
suggests that the best thing that Eve could ever have done was
to eat the apple and risk being exiled. Had she remained in the
Garden, she would have continued to be an obedient child with
God creating her life. However, in her banishment, she, at
least, lives with the opportunity to create her values and, in
doing so, begins to craft her adult life.

From this mythic perspective, we might say we have two
choices: to remain obedient in the Garden, reduced to an immature spiritual path, or desire to find our truth, which may
result in some form of separation. It is critical to note that being willing to unearth our truth is always accompanied by a
fear of separation from family, a spouse, a friend, a boss, or a
congregation.

I recall coming home from college, as a sophomore studying philosophy, and announcing to my Irish-Catholic father
that I had decided to be an atheist. He promptly replied, "I
don't give a shit what you are. When you're home, you'll go to

church with the family." To which I reacted, "Okay, I won't be coming home much." Having the last word in the exchange felt like a huge triumph. Overcoming this fear of separation or abandonment may be at the core of what it means to save ourselves.

SAVING OURSELVES

If a mature spirituality means saving ourselves, then we will need to understand what will support our choice to risk abandonment. It may be that in small acts of accountability, we develop the spiritual practice of preparing to take on the responsibility of saving ourselves. It can be as simple as admitting a mistake, apologizing, or creating restitution for some loss we caused another to suffer. Putting a stop to our blaming of others is a spiritual practice that strengthens our capacity to be self-accountable.

If being self-accountable is a primary spiritual practice, then letting go of the shame that prohibits accountability is also an essential spiritual practice. We have been offered an immense example of shame restricting self-accountability in the President we elected in 2016. Rather than remaining stuck on chastising him for such a significant failure of leadership, let his example be used by all of us to be more willing to own the shame that prevents us from being self-accountable.

The first step is to notice the eagerness we may have to explain and justify our behavior to others. These attempts at self-vindication are quite often the voice of shame. So, the first step is an increased awareness of the shame giving rise to the series of defenses we employ in support of our essential goodness. Just seeing our shame tends to mitigate it. When shame is absent, these defenses simply don't show up, the rare exception being when we have been unjustifiably accused.

The second step is to understand that we are likely carrying the shame of another. This person could have been an early authority figure who employed shame to control your behavior or a perpetrator who violated you in some way and never acknowledged the shame of his or her wrongdoing. This can result in the victim carrying the denied shame of the perpetrator.

Third, write a letter, which you don't necessarily intend to send, to the person who shamed you. In the letter, express your anger regarding how it has been for you to live with shame. Let the person know that you're giving the shame back to them because it doesn't belong to you. Add anything in your letter that supports your essential goodness.

Fourth, commit to the spiritual practice of being conscious that you are shaming yourself or diminishing yourself in some way. Make it talkable. Let a trusted other know that you are attacking yourself. Shame has difficulty sustaining itself when seen or heard. When I'm in the grips of shame, I often say to my spouse, "I've walked away from my goodness." Remember, there is no more preferred spiritual practice than the restoration of love, and that is what you're doing when you interrupt shame.

Fifth, we sometimes shame what we don't want ourselves to indulge in. I realize that I shamed my tears in childhood because it was very unlikely that I would receive the support I needed. The shame kept my tears at bay. Now, many years later, I give my tears permission, and as my eyes water, there is inevitably a hint of shame. The good news is that the permission I give that emotional expression overrides shame's power over it. Sometimes, people shame having a voice, taking some risk, or acting in any way they deem as possessing more injurious consequences than feeling shame.

Sixth, as a spiritual practice, build an evolving resiliency to reflect and not react to folks perceiving you in ways contrary to how you see yourself. When you hear an unfavorable perception someone has of you, do not talk them out of it. If you believe that feedback to be unwarranted, you might simply ask whether there is something they want from you based on their perception. If they do share some desire of you, then let yourself have the options of responding positively, rejecting the request, or negotiating.

The suggestion is that saving yourself means engaging in a spiritual practice that supports your essential goodness. Self-accountability needs to be an intimate act. Its voice needs to be: "I'm the one that made the mistake." "I welcome my feelings in regard to having made that mistake, as I feel regret, remorse, and sadness." "I want to acknowledge my mistake to whoever has been impacted by my action." "If I have difficulty holding my goodness as a result of having made this mistake, then my task is to work on forgiving myself."

The intimacy is reflected in the honesty, the willingness to know yourself and what you did, the acceptance of the feelings accompanying your admission, accessing the forgiveness you deserve, and, finally, interrupting whatever shame may be separating you from the act of being accountable.

GRATITUDE AND GENEROSITY

We can see the spirit of emotional generosity in a blessing by John O'Donohue, entitled "To Come Home to Yourself":

> May all that is unforgiven in you
> Be released.
> May your fears yield
> Their deepest tranquilities.
> May all that is unlived in you
> Blossom into a future
> Graced with love.

The essence of spiritual maturity is a level of delight sweeping through the heart when feeling gratitude and being generous. Gratitude offers the pronouncement, "I am one who receives much, and I am thankful." What happens to us when we define ourselves as appreciative receivers?

We begin to release a compulsive narcissism that has us perched, awaiting more good stuff. Of course, the ego remains insatiable. There simply isn't ever enough love, enough attention, enough admiration, and enough security. We remain caught in the ego's ravenous hunger. It's convinced that it loses its purpose if it allows for enough.

To deal with the ego's unquenchable thirst, I recommend gratitude as a daily spiritual practice. Simply pause for several minutes and call to mind what you've been given or, before you get out of bed, give thanks for the new day given to you. Initially, you may experience your gratitude inventory like an innocuous grocery list. Keep doing it! Eventually, the joy of receiving will begin to resonate with the items on your list.

If you run into difficulty by raising a question regarding your deservedness to receive, stop and consider several questions. First, does questioning your deservedness keep you loyal to someone in your past who questioned your deservedness? Second, does questioning your deservedness allow you to remain a victim? Third, does it allow you to be risk averse since a lack of deservedness implies that you're not good enough? The key is to remember that deciding you are not deserving is never true, but it does have a purpose, as suggested by the above questions.

I have noticed that my receiving of joy points toward an emerging desire to announce that I've been given a lot. It's refreshing to see that I have little or no need to compare what I have received to what others have gotten. I simply want to identify myself as an appreciative beneficiary. The feeling of gratitude then morphs into a cornerstone of personal identity.

It could be one of the greatest gifts I've given myself.

When gratitude runs through the soul, there is much less likelihood of living life as a victim. Victimization depersonalizes life and separates us from our experiences. Something or someone out there is the author of your life, and they have done you wrong. We all lapse from time to time into self-victimization. It's not like violations such as rape, muggings, and atrocities of war don't reduce us to victims. The key is to not take up residency there too long.

Victimhood is an indirect way of suggesting we deserve more, but again, enough may remain elusive. It can also be a way to remain risk avoidant: "Look at the awful stuff life's done to me. It doesn't make sense for me or anyone else to expect too much of me." It also announces that we are in protest of living life on life's terms. It can place us in an adolescent holding pattern, declaring that life is not supposed to be mysterious, insecure, and unpredictable. And yet, that appears to be the nature of the journey.

For a mature spirituality to unfold, we must be willing to live life on life's terms. It is the elder's responsibility to remain curious about what life may be asking for, even during the most challenging of times. Such a curiosity constitutes living intimately.

We've already addressed generosity, especially emotional generosity. It's too easy to view emotional generosity as occurring between people. Elders on a soulful path are recipients of their own emotional generosity. They remember that they are stewards of their worth. They remain emotionally generous as they hold the responsibility to forgive themselves. They commit to treating themselves kindly, especially attending to their emotional needs. They let themselves know when they need help and allow themselves to ask for it. They know how to remain recipients of their emotional generosity, a hallmark of spiritual maturity.

A BLESSING FOR EMOTIONAL GENEROSITY

It may be the season that calls you to keep
your promise to serve.
Somewhere in the depths of your soul,
you always knew that service was your purpose.
Allow emotional generosity to be the path of serving well.
It's time to give away your heart
since its life depends upon it.

So, it is with being emotionally generous:
the more you offer, the fuller your cup.
The courage that cuts across artificiality
unearths more of you.
Both the served and the server can feast
from the abundance of an open heart.
It's time to simply smile at distractions, freeing generosity.

Begin by slowly releasing your grip on pretense.
You are emotionally generous when you risk being here.
Some vulnerable feeling comes out of hiding,
and you utter "I'm scared," or "I love you."
Authenticity held in compassion reveals a bounty
of emotional generosity.

We are each waiting to be benevolently witnessed.
There is immense generosity in such witnessing.
It is the welcome most desired.
It says, "You are not alone; I am with you."
The generous moment of witness releases striving
as you relax into yourself.
In this moment, there's nowhere to go.

Release the question,
"Should I forgive the one who hurt me?"
You are deeply emotionally generous
when you call yourself an apprentice to forgiveness.

Knowing all the while that some offering of forgiveness
depends on how much you're willing to forgive yourself.
Be curious and kind in your apprenticeship.

As you live your emotional generosity,
life will not have forgotten you.
Those who waited to be fed will bless your gift again and again.
As much as you are touched by their appreciation,
your generosity has released you from insisting
that life has forsaken you.
Your union with life is woven by the one who gives.

IDENTITY CRISIS

I was eager to continue my conversation with Emma regarding a mature spirituality. Although I had taught comparative religion, I had avoided using the word *spiritual* most of my life. Not because I didn't believe it had its place when considering human development, but because I feared being associated with something too virtuous or devout. There was something about aging that seemed to offer me more permission to explore spirituality. I decided to tell Emma about my lifelong reluctance to address spirituality and the current changes in my attitude.

"For sure, you would have resisted identifying yourself as interested in spirituality. You've been very clear about having been raised by Scotch-Irish rogues who held disdain for anyone suggesting they were deserving of reverence," Emma pointed out, appearing satisfied to connect who I am to where I come from, and I liked that she remembered.

"I think you're right. There was no room in the family I come from for anything sounding a bit arrogant. However, I don't think that any reference to spirituality had to imply that I'm without sin," I surmised, feeling some relief from the fear of being perceived as righteous.

"I'm hearing your interest in what might be a mature spiritual path, which has nothing to do with being self-righteous. Should we continue?" Emma asked, aware of my sensitivity about being perceived as self-righteous, making me a bit suspicious about those who worry so much about it.

"Absolutely. It feels like the cornerstone of a soulful path to elderhood," I offered.

"Living a mature spirituality will be marked by an identity crisis, which accompanies any significant life transition such as eldering," asserted Emma, once again displaying comfort with something so uncomfortable as a crisis.

"I thought that an identity crisis only happened to younger men! Why would the possibility of moving into a more mature spirituality involve a crisis of any kind?" I wondered, hoping I had misunderstood her.

"Do you know the original definition of the word *religion*?" asked Emma.

"I think that the definition is 'to reconnect,'" I suggested.

"Yes, it is 'to reconnect.' But to reconnect to what?"

"I'm thinking to reconnect to ourselves, maybe in a new way," I said, hoping that my speculation would be close to her vision.

"Absolutely. We reconnect to ourselves, and as we do so, we honor the essence of life, which is impermanence or change. We don't pretend that we are something static or inanimate. That's a deeply spiritual act, to reconnect to ourselves in a new way, suggesting we are allowing life to teach us and create us," Emma explained, settling back into her chair, offering a measure of confidence with her declaration.

"I'm not sure what the reconnection would look like, and is it an identity crisis?" I wondered, feeling assured that Emma would be willing to work gently with my confusion.

"Reconnecting and not reconnecting is the real identity

crisis. It's similar to a trapeze artist who has let go of the bar and is twirling through space in the hope of receiving a pair of clasping hands, securing her flight in her partner's grip," Emma pointed out.

"The analogy helps me. When I am in an identity crisis, I'm no longer swinging from the original bar, and I haven't reached the other side comfortably. Could the original bar be something like a belief I've been carrying?" I asked, feeling as if I might be making some headway with this talk of an identity crisis.

"Sure, it could be a belief, a vision, a habit, a relationship, or a value you've lived by, and you're releasing it—or, at least, releasing your dependence on it. It may simply mean allowing a belief to have less influence over your decisions. The key is to not rush your movement to the other side. Be patient; support your rhythm and timing. Of course, flying through midair is frightening. When you let go of whatever has supported your identity, like the platform the trapeze artist stands on, you'll get scared. None of us want to be strangers to ourselves, but that's what happens when we stand on the platform with the trapeze bar in our hands without letting go. We wear out old ways of identifying ourselves. We know they no longer work, but we allow fear to keep us where we don't belong, refusing to reconnect—that is, not allowing ourselves to be truly religious, if you will," concluded Emma, leaving me feeling the assistance offered by the analogy.

"Staying with the analogy, is there a net?"

"Of course, the net is your support system, and when you fall, your identity is temporarily confirmed as the one being held by those who love you," added Emma with a smile, suggesting she knew a bit about falling into the net.

"I find the image very comforting. And I really like the idea that a mature spirituality is living religiously by reconnecting to ourselves with the refinement of beliefs, values, and decisions. I'm assuming that the hope is in the heart and wisdom we bring to our reconnecting," I said, starting to understand the relationship between an identity crisis and eldering.

"Sure, because we are ultimately reconnecting to others, nature, and the impenetrable mystery of God, as well as to ourselves. The hope is that the reconnecting possesses a bit more faith and love for the mysteries of the self, others, nature, and God," offered Emma.

"This is very helpful for me. I'm starting to see that my crisis of identity is an opportunity for a religious experience. My hunch is that I'm being asked to engage in reconnecting how I carry and steward my gifts," I concluded.

"That sounds right. Give it some reflection and remain mindful that reconnecting to your gifts may be about what it means not to be overly attached to them," Emma advised, leaning forward as a gesture of emphasis.

LOOSENING AN ATTACHMENT TO THE GIFTS

Emma's appeal to not be overly attached to my gifts remained with me. I could feel its importance regarding a mature spirituality. Of course, the initial consideration is to be clear about the nature of one's gifts. It could be a trade, an expertise, or a mastery of some kind.

Once I identified my gifts, I wanted to understand what might get me overly attached to my gifts and what might be the consequence of an over-attachment. It appeared that a strong influential factor in getting overly attached to my gifts might be the recognition and admiration that comes with offering the gifts.

Recently, I was asked to offer a presentation of Joseph Campbell's "The Hero's Journey." Afterward, a young man said of me, "He's like a classical pianist who's asked to play a

Mozart piece and, with no hesitation, quickly produces the piece." I felt thankful for the recognition and needed to remind myself that my worth is not determined by receiving admiration, though I could feel my ego primed to receive more.

CONSEQUENCES OF BEING OVERLY ATTACHED TO YOUR GIFTS

Prone to inflation. When identity rests strongly upon the gifts, it becomes too easy to bring a measure of aggrandizement to who we are.

A vision of our humanity can be compromised. It can become difficult to see who we are beyond the gifts, especially the fumbling and character flaws.

It can be difficult to see the gifts of others. It's easy to get somewhat myopic, preoccupied with our gifts, and prone to compare and diminish the gifts of others.

Self-worth runs the risk of being conditional. It's also easy to see our value as dependent on the successful delivery of our gifts and the favorable responses of recipients.

Prone to resenting others when they don't respond favorably to our offerings. When either the gifts don't have an opportunity to be offered or they are simply not received well by others, this results in confusion about who we are.

Susceptible to an identity crisis. This issue is highly prevalent among anyone receiving large degrees of public acclaim, such as professional athletes and movie stars.

The dilemma. When your gifts are carrying much of the weight of your identity, significant emotional pressure ensues to demonstrate that the next offering will even be bigger, better, and more impressive than the last. This dilemma easily translates into significant burnout.

GETTING LESS ATTACHED

Remaining mindful of seduction. Admiration can be seductive and in need of mindfulness to have options regarding a relationship with one's gifts.

It was given to you. Acknowledge that the gifts we possess were given to us, bestowed upon us genetically. Mentors and teachers likely made valuable contributions along the way. This keeps the gifts less about you.

Feeling gratitude for what was given to you. Gratitude is a wonderful correction for aggrandizement, allowing us to be responsible for stewarding the gifts and allowing the gifts to serve others.

Taking responsibility for exercising our best discernment regarding where the gifts can best serve. This means being alert to unthinkingly bringing the gifts to where there is the greatest degree of praise, getting lost in being impressive rather than clear about where the gifts can best serve.

Remembering that your gifts are not above refinement.

Remaining devoted to the essential task of eldering, which is blessing the gifts of younger people and serving wherever possible.

Recommitting to holding unconditional love for yourself.

The light attachment to your gifts doesn't mean you should ignore the gifts. It simply means the gifts do not inordinately define who you are. Ultimately, remaining vigilant about loosening your attachment to your gifts is a wonderful ego correction in support of a mature spirituality.

SUFFERING

"You brought some clarity to what it means to be over-identified with your gifts," suggested Emma, smiling with what I hoped was satisfaction.

"Yes, I'm feeling much more comfortable with what it means to be over-identified with my gifts, the consequences, and how to mitigate an over-identification. I'm assuming that we covered the nature of a mature spirituality," I concluded, hoping for Emma's agreement.

"Well, let's see what we've covered. As you just mentioned, there's avoiding over-identification with your gifts, there's learning to save yourself, and there's allowing gratitude and generosity to guide your thinking and your choices. There's also learning to navigate an identity crisis. Well, I think the only thing left is suffering," explained Emma, emphasizing that last word with a somewhat cavalier attitude.

"Suffering! You're saying that suffering is an essential component of a mature spirituality? It sounds a bit masochistic," I teased, not certain where she was going.

"Oh, no, not masochistic at all. It's just that suffering offers a very large story about who you are, the nature of the human condition, and life itself. Besides, it is the second-largest common denominator that connects all of us," returned Emma.

"What's the largest common denominator?"

"Mortality," offered Emma with a very casual demeanor.

"I get it. I need to hear more about the large stories

brought forth by suffering," I added, confident that Emma could easily take me there.

"Sure. Let's start with an old definition of the word *suffering*, which is 'to allow, to permit, to bear, and to endure.' I especially like 'to allow and to permit,'" described Emma, allowing etymology to direct the inquiry.

"When I hear you reference the large story advanced by suffering, it sounds like you're saying suffering is a good thing, which I have trouble accepting," I quipped.

"Of course. See if you can approach suffering by suspending 'good' and 'bad.' Those categories just won't be very helpful in understanding something like suffering. Try using categories like natural, necessary, and even genuine," rejoined Emma, offering a novel perspective on suffering.

"Genuine! I think I understand natural and necessary, but I'm not sure about genuine," I admitted, realizing I was banging into my reluctance to pursue the topic.

"Well, if the suffering is real, then the person will be without pretense and as genuine as humanly possible," Emma explained.

"I see. Can we talk more about how the natural and necessary suffering offer large stories?" I asked, now authentically curious about where the inquiry would take us.

"Sure. Keep in mind the old definition of the word *suffering*, which is 'to allow' or 'to permit.' Now, let's add a quote by John Keats found in his letters: 'Do you not see how necessary a world of pains and troubles is to school an intelligence and make it a soul?' He's saying that suffering can educate your intelligence and make it a soul," asserted Emma with a confidence that made even me feel comfortable while continuing to feel bewildered, me hoping I might sound intelligent in my response.

"Well, it certainly sounds like making my intelligence a soul would support a soulful path to elderhood," I speculated in the hope that I was at least bringing two congruent concepts together.

"Yes, that's true. However, let's begin by noting that Keats is suggesting that suffering can school or educate an intelligence. What do you imagine an uneducated intelligence might look like?" invited Emma, stimulating in me a more robust interest in the notion of an uneducated intelligence.

"That's a great question. I'm assuming the last thing an uneducated intelligence needs is formal education. I'm thinking that an uneducated intelligence would likely be an immature intelligence," I offered, glad to see Emma nodding in the affirmative before I finished the sentence.

"Sure, that's a great way to look at it. So, what are your thoughts about an immature intelligence?" invited Emma, knowing I was eager to explore.

"My hunch is that an immature intelligence is not formed by instinct, emotion, and imagination. If anything, it's with a great deal of curiosity. An immature intelligence is quite content generating an endless string of abstract concepts. What comes to mind is that an immature intelligence is trying not to live life on life's terms. It is as if a person could simply define life with a variety of ideas and not face the risks that real participation calls for," I claimed, feeling good about my understanding.

"Yes, yes. An immature intelligence wants to hide behind a shield of abstraction. Can you see what suffering is capable of doing to the shield?" reckoned Emma, leaving me ready to consider suffering in a new way.

"I think so. Suffering hurls me into life on life's terms. It can be too difficult to pretend that figuring something out is going to benefit me. I might even admit that life is incredibly larger than me. When you're right in the midst of suffering, it's damn difficult to pretend that you're something that you're not," I added passionately, veiling the lack of application I possessed concerning my understanding.

"As I hear you, I'm thinking of the bout with Ménière's disease that came roaring down into your life about a year ago," offered Emma, her gaze and voice softening.

"Yes, it was just a year ago when I looked up away from the computer screen, only to be sent to the floor by an immense rush of vertigo. With some help from my wife, I was able to crawl to a nearby couch, where I laid for six hours spinning, vomiting, and retching. I finally rolled over onto the floor, and while keeping my chin no more than six inches above the rug, I crawled to the bedroom. There were only three or four more episodes of severe vertigo. However, there have been numerous incidents of dizziness and low-grade physical instability. I conferred with a neurologist, a hearing expert in Chicago, and another in Boston. My visits yielded no prognosis or a plan to support remission. I slowly began to accept that I had been hurled into a significant depth of mystery by this condition. It began to feel like it had much more control over my life than I did," I said.

"I spent some time denying it, protesting it, and feeling damn victimized by it," I added, pausing to allow a stream of vulnerability to move up through my chest and into my throat as I gently began to sob.

I felt embraced by the silence and much less afraid of a vulnerability that was residing in my heart and had become more compelling throughout the past year.

"You've been learning about suffering. If you're up to it, I'd love to hear more about how you've been 'schooling your intelligence,'" invited Emma, as if cradling an element of faith in my devotion to the inquiry.

"I acknowledge how much I don't know about life. Its immensity and mystery are much more apparent to me now. The idea of who's serving who is much clearer. I've spent so long believing on some level that life was supposed to serve me, which embarrasses me to admit. But it's true. I get that I'm responsible for serving life," I confided, the words leaving my lips with a hesitation, reflecting their first attempt to be audible.

"Paul, what does serving life look like for you?" asked Emma, leaving me feeling grateful for a much-needed focus.

"Well, for me, it doesn't mean becoming an ascetic. I mostly want to know where it is that my gifts can make the most significant offering. And that doesn't necessarily mean where there is the biggest or most dramatic social or economic context. It means remaining discerning regarding who is asking for what I have to give, who's ready and willing to receive. Sometimes, I serve by making anonymous offerings to where there is an obvious need. It mostly means living the question of where and whom I serve. I want to die with the belief that I served well. Yeah, that is important to me," I concluded, glad to tell this story of service.

"That's a pretty large suffering story," added Emma.

"Yes, I guess it is. I would have to be out to lunch, unable to see what Ménière's disease is saying about who serves who. I get that life is not supposed to serve me. Actually, l enjoy letting go of all the drama that ensues when I decide that life is not doing a good job serving me. There's just too much of me in that old story," I replied, feeling the weight of self-pity and protest when life has not made an appropriate delivery.

"Of course, suffering has difficulty satisfying the task of 'schooling an intelligence' if we fall into a victim's posture as a result of suffering," explained Emma, reiterating the consequences of leaning into being a victim.

"For sure, that went on for a while. My protesting got very tiring, and I decided if Victor Frankl could endure a concentration camp by asking, 'What is this experience asking of me?' then I should be able to ask that about my condition," I said, feeling an element of competition with Frankl and scared I might lose.

"I do want you to know that I am saddened by you being asked to endure this condition, and I respect your willingness to live the question regarding what it may be asking of you. That question allows you to walk away from experiencing the affliction as simply unfortunate. I would love to hear more about how you've been responding to the question," implored Emma, her interest palpable.

"Well, it has become obvious that it is quite challenging for me to honor my limits. I'm deeply curious about the part of me that's into dishonoring his limits," I admitted, feeling a solid receptivity to exploring the question.

"Let yourself find him in the moment. My guess is that he is close by," invited Emma, her words drifting in the air like a breeze, able to open a door for my exploration.

"I think he might be the part of me that only knows how to hold conditional love for myself. If I honor my limits, then I might have to pause and interrupt the project of demonstrating that I'm lovable. How would I even know that I'm okay? As I tell you, I can feel the fatigue of such a grind and the absurdity that enough nifty achievements are even possible to illustrate my deservedness. God, I hate to admit it, but normally I would not pay attention to fatigue or not feeling well as indicators that my limits may be asking to be accepted. But the price I pay now under the shadow of Ménière's feels like a bit too much to continue disregarding limits. Maybe it's this condition that is inviting me to consider offering myself unconditional love," I uttered, surprised by my words, feeling the pretense of knowing how to talk about the issue while being in the dark.

"Do you dare say it? Has suffering made you more self-loving?" asked Emma, her appreciation for my awareness quite apparent.

"I do feel more deserving of rest, play, attention, and

support. That feels like I'm being more loving. My suffering reminds me of the suffering of others. I can, on a good day, summon more compassion for others, knowing that we travel together down the road of suffering. Also, sometimes I feel how tight of a grip I have on the steering wheel while I'm driving, such that the simple act of loosening my hands feels loving. I have lived a demanding life, demands that hurled me onto a quest for proving, demonstrating, and even attempting to save others," I added, noting a feeling of melancholy as well as pretense accompanying my novice-level knowing.

"I sense something is touching you. Do you know what it is?" asked Emma.

"No, I'm not sure. It feels like sadness."

"Take your time. Close your eyes and see if you can locate the sadness in your body and offer it an invitation," Emma gently encouraged, leading me to feel very receptive to her invitation.

I felt witnessed and emotionally held by Emma. It was easy for me to just be with the melancholy. It was a gift to pause in the truth of this feeling. I slowly opened my eyes, tears streaming down my cheeks.

"I don't know anything about feeling unconditional love for myself. Last Friday, I woke at 4:00 AM and laid in bed perseverating in thought about all there was to do. The stress of these reflections left me physically unstable. Two hours later, I laid on the couch, dizzy, retching, and vomiting. Sometimes, I can step away from the inner demands; other times, they take over with an unbridled tenacity," I shared, feeling a comforting relief in welcoming this depth of honesty.

We spent the rest of our meeting working with a much younger version of myself who believed he had failed to save his parents and his brother. That alleged failure transitioned into a devotion to saving the world, which did not feel grandiose at all when driven by the magical thinking of a nine-year-old.

I left Emma's that day a bit clearer about unnecessary suffering created by an extremely heroic undertaking. I realized that Emma was correct in identifying my condition as an element of the Trials and Ordeals comprising the second stage of my Initiation into eldering. By the time I reached home, I felt deeply curious about whether or not unconditional love might be an offering to myself. It felt like a real problem since I could deeply feel its importance to a soulful path to elderhood.

HUMILITY:
Unconditional Love for the Self

Several conversations with two of my colleagues began to shed light on the possibility of unconditional self-love. Typically, I have heard unconditional love being mentioned only when someone was seeking relief from the burden of pursuing elusive conditional self-love. It seems easy to understand that conditions are unceasing. One follows the other with a growing sense of urgency and demand to succeed and achieve with no hope of the efforts realizing completion. Each opportunity to demonstrate one's deservedness simply provides a chance to succeed or fail at the attempt, with success being but a fleeting moment of affectionate reprieve.

I've heard reference to the divine spark possessed at birth when the focus turns to what it means to deserve unconditional love. I find myself comfortable with such a suggestion and also feeling wanting. Does the recommendation suggest we should remain mindful of our divine origin? What does it take to live with such mindfulness? Does it make sense to believe that the goodness possessed at birth is the same one lived with now? Do I continue to be worthy of unconditional love when engaging in obvious immoral actions—that is, behavior clearly in violation of my core values?

These curiosities led me to believe that we may carry that original divine deservedness and that we are quite different as adults. I kept wondering whether there might be something more able to point us at least in the direction of unconditional love for the self. My conversations and reflections began to reveal humility as a possible answer.

I decided that one way to understand humility was as the gracious acceptance of our limits, often accompanied by a hint of melancholy. I could see that the acceptance was about love. The very idea that it is about loving our limits and accepting our shortcomings suggested it was without conditions. Humility is certainly a way to interrupt the ego's propensity for aggrandizement. From the ego's perspective, we are never quite big enough. Thus, we are condemned to conditional self-love. Humility offers an invitation to who we are: the heartbreaks, the strengths, the weaknesses, the mistakes, and the times we acted with contempt.

I include a hint of melancholy in my understanding of humility, reflecting the forlorn response to the unlived dreams of a refined version of the self. Humility tends to be a veiled virtue. It may be difficult to know when we are in the presence of someone humble. We may also not witness our humility. Its delicate nature may be due to its nuanced residency between arrogance and false modesty. It may be helpful to look at some common characteristics of false modesty and arrogance to gain some clarity about where humility lives. Here are some typical descriptions:

False Modesty	Arrogance
Servile	Demanding
Self-doubting	Over-confident
Reticent	Aggressive
Self-effacing	Boastful
Deferential	Excessively Entitled
Demure	Flamboyant

False modesty tends to be an underprivileged way to love the self. Arrogance is an over-privileged way to demonstrate an elusive deservedness of love for the self. False modesty is quite often the result of having a strong adverse reaction to the possibility of being arrogant or being perceived by others as arrogant. False modesty is also employed as a strategic interpersonal defense. The energetic message sent to others is "There's no need to feel threatened by me. I'm no threat to you at all because there's not enough of me to be threatening."

False modesty is often viewed as "cute" and can be confused with genuine humility. It's too easy to enable falsely modest folks because they don't pose much of a threat to getting a variety of our needs met. It can be enjoyable to benefit from their deferential nature. Arrogance, on the other hand, tends to catch a bad rap because there is a shortage of advantages being in the presence of arrogance.

What appears to be most noteworthy is that once either false modesty or arrogance is deemed inappropriate and unacceptable, we naturally compensate and find ourselves housed in the other dynamic. Thus, those of us who do our best not to succumb to arrogance find ourselves held in the grip of false modesty under the illusion that all is well. Only through increased levels of humility can we hope to avoid this compensatory maneuver. Humility offers the opportunity to accept how human it is to wander into either false modesty or arrogance.

False modesty or having a deflated sense of self can be appropriate. I found recently, when we lost our beloved Golden Retriever, that my grief had me saying less, feeling less entitled, and feeling disinterested in taking risks. I was living with a smaller version of myself, which could be viewed as false modesty.

And so, there are times when an inflated sense of self or arrogance might be generative or helpful in some way. I recall several years ago speaking with a mentor of mine about some regret I had over a recent display of arrogance. He leaned forward and said, "Didn't you recently meet with the principal of the local high school and inform her that you wanted to start a mentoring community with a group of ninth-grade boys?" I nodded in the affirmative, to which he responded, "Sounds damn arrogant to me!" I left with the understanding that it may serve a worthy purpose to occasionally get inflated. We can simply accept a propensity for both, seeing how each may be helpful at times, as well as making whatever corrections one needs to step back in the direction of humility.

An old definition of the word *humble* is "on the ground." We can say that an essential mark of humility is to be grounded. We can think of grounded as non-dramatic or non-reactionary. "On the ground" might suggest a gracious acceptance of limitations, which naturally morphs into a proclivity for self-forgiveness. There is a quality of emotional stability where there is an openness to the views of others without being excessively influenced. There is an ease in noticing the need for help and asking for it. There is as much value attributed to listening as there is to having a voice. There is also a non-heroic response to what life presents, accepting one's limits. There is a commitment to live by taking discerned risks. Lastly, there is a willingness to stumble into false modesty or arrogance, avoiding a compensatory process. Here's what the list might look like:

HUMILITY

- Grounded and non-dramatic
- Responsive rather than reactionary
- Accepting of personal limits
- Valuing listening as well as speaking
- Exercising an ease in acknowledging the achievements of others

- Emotional stability
- Being able to identify a need for help and ask for it
- Permission to be both falsely modest and arrogant
- Committed to being self-forgiving

These characteristics likely reveal how close we can get to holding unconditional love for the self.

A BLESSING FOR HUMILITY

When humble, you're standing on the ground,
not trying to be more or less than who you are.
Of course, trying to be more or less are attempts to not be here,
in one single place on the ground.
Humility is a courageous act of welcome.
What shines and what is tattered are not hidden,
but rather revealed and witnessed,
leaving you at peace with yourself.

From the place you stand, you are responsive and not reactionary.
The former is informed by what dwells in your soul
and not from what gains external notoriety.
Instinct, deep sentiment, and reflection constellate,
telling you how to be yourself while you engage what approaches.
This ability to be responsive
gives testimony to your being grounded in integrity.

Under the light of humility, your limits are neither overly embraced,
providing a place to hide, nor pushed and cajoled toward
    transcendence.
Rather, they are the shape and contour of who you are now.
With an act of genuine acceptance,
they germinate into possibility.
What originally appeared to diminish you
ends an incubation and births a dream.

Humility does not ask to keep your head abidingly bowed.
Rather, it encourages you to bow to your own humanity and,
thus unfolds an ease in bowing to the humanity of others.
Humility does not require absence but rather
your full participation as an imperfect person,
stumbling toward enlightenment and learning to bow to the
   pilgrimage.

Humility is not to be achieved.
It is meant to be the recipient of your devotion.
You will notice some tendency to inflate yourself,
only to notice a compensatory move to then deflate.
Humility asks that you allow these slips and tendencies to
simply reflect the vibrancy and oscillation of personality.
Just continue to devotionally hold your limits and foibles.

Humility mostly asks that you remember it
as a tender and gentle shoot of love.
Humility remembers how fragile, vulnerable,
and divine you were at birth.
All that remains the same, with the addition of freedom and
   responsibility.
Now, you are capable of triumph and defeat.
Open your heart and welcome the incompleteness of your
   personhood.

I decided to review the elements of a mature spirituality before returning to Emma's. I felt thankful for all we covered under the auspices of a maturing spirituality. There was the notion of saving ourselves, which was especially important for me, as I was only too ready to attempt to save someone else. The emphasis we placed on self-accountability and interrupting the shame that might interfere with being accountable went a long way in support of my individuation.

I especially appreciated the roles of gratitude and emotional generosity. I found myself turning to them any time I felt lost on the path to eldering. I appreciated being able to hold an identity crisis as simply a measure of growth and change rather than a statement of my inadequacy. Learning to loosen my attachment to my gifts and remain an apprentice to suffering helped me be less heroic and more accepting of the learning that comes by way of challenges. Lastly, to see humility as the best approach to unconditional love for the self was an immense gift.

I had to remind myself not to let pride get in the way as I was guided now by Emma. I opened to her guidance by calling to mind that I had never been an elder in this lifetime and could use all the help I could get. I also recalled how, at the age of twenty-nine, I was first mentored by John and Joyce. My pride began to recede as I felt deep gratitude for having been guided along the way.

12: GETTING READY TO TRANSITION

"The only way death is not meaningless is to see yourself as part of something greater: a family, a community, a society."

– Atul Gawande

I arrived at Emma's feeling fulfilled about our work related to a maturing spirituality, especially the focus on humility. It was hard for me to imagine what else a soulful path to elderhood might be asking for.

"We've said a great deal about the nature of a soulful path to elderhood," I offered, hoping we had covered it all while not wanting to leave anything out.

"Yes, I feel quite positive about our work. And there is another important focus," suggested Emma.

"What's that?" I asked, wondering how much else could there possibly be.

"It's about what it means to get ready to transition," added Emma.

"Transition to what?" I wondered.

"Transition to the end of your life and the other side. You know, death and dying," retorted Emma, not concealing her chagrin.

"Yes, I get it. I just never thought about it in terms of transitioning. I mean, transitioning suggests that there's movement from one place to another. How would I know where I'm going when I die?" I asked, hoping the conversation was not about to get lost in celestial musing.

"Paul, did you ever really know where you were going? For example, in the roles you played, did you ever know where you were going as a spouse, father, friend, teacher, and healer? You were always stepping into some measure of mystery. We're just talking about stepping into more mystery in death than you're accustomed to in life," explained Emma in her casual way, as if dying was not very different from any other life experience.

"You sound like there is something rather than nothing in the mystery of death," I pointed out somewhat argumentatively, feeling unreceptive to being influenced regarding the nature of the afterlife.

"And you believe nothing about death is mysterious?" wondered Emma, leading me to believe she had made peace with the mystery of death.

"I was going to say that I'm not sure. However, I've never known a transition where there was nothing on the other side. Maybe I do believe there is a mysterious something on the other side of dying," I said, actually coming into the idea as I spoke, hardly believing my ears.

"The ego abhors excessive mystery. It acts as if there's nothing if it doesn't know about it. The ego strives to hold its alleged prowess regarding knowing," described Emma.

"I feel comfortable with the idea that following death, there's a mysterious something. So, how do I get ready for this mysterious something?" I inquired with a note of sarcasm escaping my lips before I could call it back.

"I recommend you start with an inventory of regrets," suggested Emma, holding a tutorial tone.

"Doesn't that imply somehow my life was simply unfortunate?" I reacted.

"No, no, it doesn't imply that you lived an unfortunate life.

Spend time with your regrets and see where they take you," Emma encouraged, and I complied in the faith that Emma knew where to begin.

REGRETS

I took Emma's recommendation and began exploring my regrets. I initially wanted to clarify what regret is. I could see regret representing disappointment and even sorrow. I wasn't sure how such an inventory would help prepare me more for my transition, but I was willing to take it on. What I call trivial regrets came to mind first, like my never making it to the NBA and not winning the lottery. I could see that some regrets were about choices I made, while others occurred due to what life presented to me along the way. I also began to see that, to a great degree, my regrets reflected my dreams. I wondered about the dreamer.

My dreams carried the spirit of my wishes, hopes, and aspirations. I began to see that my dreams were also my way of loving life. They were a kind of declaration: "Okay, life, this is what I want from you and what I want to do. I want us to collaborate and co-create." Sometimes, I was acquainted with the dream before life stepped in and either cooperated or took me somewhere I was unprepared to go. Other times, I only knew the dream because life provided unexpected detours.

Some of these unexpected diversions included failing off the basketball team in college, having a daughter die two days after birth, and raising another daughter who was born severely disabled. I certainly had responsibility for my academic floundering, while the other two deviations from the dream path appear to have occurred due to the will of fate.

I began to wonder what these regrets might be asking for. Each provided me with varying degrees of loss and sorrow.

The death of the athletic dream was easier to unpack. While going to college to play basketball, acquiring a degree was simply an extra benefit. Not being able to play and not wanting to be drafted into the military made my academic career more attractive. Due to the encouragement of my roommate, I began taking courses in philosophy, ultimately majoring in it and eventually teaching it.

I began to see how regret could reveal more of the depth and breadth of my lived experience. It seemed appropriate to hold the loss of a basketball career while acknowledging what the loss issued to me. Regret had the power to display more of life than I had imagined.

I wondered what regret related to the death of one daughter and the disability of another might reveal. They both reflected the deviation of a dream that included a major part of life. There was the loss of witnessing their development, the relationships that they would have created, defeats and triumphs, grandchildren, and the deep satisfaction of accompanying them heartfully. Of course, Sarah and I do share some compromised version of the dream. But what of Kirsten, the infant who died: Could that be a situation where there was anything but unfortunate loss?

That unfortunate loss remains with me. I was a golden boy in my twenties, convinced that whatever I dreamed could be manifested without hesitation. Dreaming was experiencing an overhaul. The death of naïveté was asking me to grieve the loss of a daughter while supporting the life of our three-year-old son—a task I was ill-equipped for, protested, and eventually accepted as part of my destiny. A mentor offered the following invitation and challenge to my maturation when he said, "Life asks you to dream, become deeply disillusioned due to some unfortunate loss, and dream again." Sometimes, it is only too easy to spend a disproportionate amount of time indulging in disillusionment. I find that the way out is to be willing to interrupt my grip on self-pity.

I continue to hold regret about Sarah's disability and increasingly ask what that loss is requesting of me. It seems to call me to the beauty of the person beyond the obvious limitations. Of course, once Sarah's beauty is more obvious, so is my beauty beyond my shortcomings and achievements alike. Sarah offers me a window into reality not distorted by the aggrandizement of my ego. She presents a deeper texture to simplicity, kindness, patience, and what it means to hold a vision of building a bridge where there is diversity.

Regret reflects the willingness to dream. Regret offers an opportunity to learn from the inevitability of loss. Regret offers the chance for soulful deepening as dreams die, ensuring significant disillusionment and the search for the courage to dream again. Getting honest about regrets reveals a larger story of the life we have lived and the one we had hoped to live.

The Danish philosopher Søren Kierkegaard suggested that we only know ourselves in retrospect. Thus, regrets can inform us about who we were and who we are. In that awareness, we can make ready for our transition.

Lastly, regrets can call us to take action by communicating some regret related to how you treated someone. I'm partial to sending cards and letters wherein I describe the behavior I believe had an unfavorable impact on someone, expressing my sorrow for the choice. There is also communication that can mitigate unnecessary regrets. This entails forwarding a message of thanks or gratitude to someone whose offering significantly benefited me.

TOUCHED BY WONDER

"I came across a quote by Helen Luke. Are you acquainted with her work?" I asked.

"Oh yes, she wrote a wonderful book on the topic of aging. What quote got your interest?" asked Emma.

"Luke says, 'So, when after having made every effort to understand, we are ready to take upon ourselves the mystery of things, then the most trivial of happenings is touched by wonder, and there may come to us, by grace, a moment of un-clouded vision.' The words keep talking to me, even though I'm not sure what she is actually saying," I continue.

"You're right. These are powerful words. Well, let's look at it together. What do you think about the importance of making every effort to understand?" invited Emma.

"You know, my first reaction was: Why make 'every effort to understand' if what we are supposed to do is be 'ready to take upon ourselves the mystery of things?'" I wondered.

"Well, for one thing, the ego must exercise its best efforts at establishing itself as greatly knowledgeable. It certainly may get a bit arrogant. However, it is also a critical way to individ-uate, to give claim to our own beliefs without simply carrying convictions held by parents, friends, churches, and schools. It also can give testimony to our devotion to living a self-exam-ining life. We remain the author of an endless series of inquir-ies. We demonstrate that we don't move with a cavalier atti-tude about understanding life and ourselves," explained Emma, her detailed focus illuminating how I might make greater peace with mystery.

"I like what you say about not having a cavalier attitude. I see how my curiosity makes a strong statement about caring. It can be a way of living intimately, as I desire to understand my experience and those folks I encounter along the way," I added.

"Yes, it can be quite intimate. Your curiosity communi-cates to the gods that you want to understand what was cre-ated and given to you. Without completely letting go of curi-osity, your efforts begin to yield a larger knowing: namely, that the truth will be much larger than all your conclusions. Then, with enough humility, you're ready to take on the mystery of things, which simply means you loosen your grip upon calculating, analyzing, formularizing, and figuring. Now, you are ready to be touched by wonder as the most trivial of happenings make their way to you," offered Emma, her tone reassuring me that I was listening to someone who knew how to do it.

"I think that I understand, and I'm asking if I really want the 'most trivial of happenings' to create wonder in me," I suggested, concerned that I might get overwhelmed with life's trivialities.

"Maybe a better phrasing for you would be the 'simplicity of happenings,' which can vividly reveal some aspect of mystery. And the word *wonder* is related to wonderful and marvelous, which are strong responses of the heart. Is that helpful?" asked Emma, her head tilting over her right shoulder.

"Yes, I see how I can become more receptive when I release a level of intensity and urgency related to something I want to understand. I've been more receptive to watching the birds at the bird feeder. How does the male cardinal know to feed his female partner? And how do the doves decide to be partners? And how do they all know when and where migration is supposed to happen? I see the warmth of greetings and welcomes in an embrace or the simple gesture of a hand on a shoulder. These days, I see so many expressions of kindness that I would have minimized in the past. The other evening in the middle of dinner, my wife turned to me and said, 'You have touched many.' I didn't refute or try to deflect the statement. I took a breath and welcomed her truth without attempting to evaluate how accurate it was. A friend said to me last week, 'I want to hear how you and I might be viewed as different as well as what we share.' The simplicity of the statement opened a door to further deepening of our relationship," I offered, realizing that my examples were significantly connected to my days with Emma.

"I think you understand how the wonderful can begin to live in simple experiences. That's what being touched by wonder means. And it is a great way to get ready to transition. You allowed yourself to receive the many simple offerings of what can be described as wonderful. I believe that is what Kathleen Dowling Singh means when she writes 'Meaning begins to go beyond the connotation of interpretation and into the experience of value.' We might say that wonder or wonderful is the 'experience of value,'" replied Emma with a softness in her cheeks and a gentle smile indicating satisfaction.

"Okay, what about the gift of 'a moment of unclouded vision,' and how does grace make that happen?" I asked with unbridled eagerness.

"I think of grace as the beauty of an unanticipated gift. Think of the receptivity you hold when being less demanding of your investigations, less bent on demonstrating how much you know. It is such receptivity that makes you ready to receive a beautiful gift, such as a moment of unclouded vision," explained Emma, leaning forward—a gesture I've come to know as an invitation to a larger truth.

"I don't want to appear to be demanding, but I'm not sure that I've been gifted by 'a moment of unclouded vision,'" I said, hoping my alleged entitlement to such a gift might go unnoticed.

"Actually, just the other day, I heard that you had been gifted by a moment of unclouded vision. You told me that you came into the awareness that neither you nor anyone really fears taking a risk. Rather, that the real fear is how we treat ourselves if there is an unfavorable outcome to the risk. I would suggest that that is a moment of unclouded vision," concluded Emma, reminding me about how much she tracked what I said.

I laughed and told Emma that my ego was ready for many moments of unclouded vision. We both began to laugh, remembering that the soulful path to elderhood is a great deal about affectionately laughing at the ego's many projects, similar to a child who views the use of magic as boundless.

PRAYERFUL SEDUCTION

Emma suggested that individuation was an extremely important endeavor in one's preparation for transitioning. It means not leaving the planet pretending we are someone other than who we are, nor regretting who we are. Individuating means living close to ourselves, honoring what we feel, believe, and value. It means being devoted to being ourselves. Joseph Campbell said, "The privilege of a lifetime is being who you are." The process can be informed by our dreams, remaining self-examining, and getting feedback from trusted others who are willing to tell us things that might be difficult to hear.

Individuating is a great deal about being internally referenced, not in some narcissistic way but rather by being less distracted by others and external events. Individuating is also about remaining responsible for our essential worth, mindful of when we are allowing someone else to do the job.

When I asked her about how to go about securing a commitment to remain individuating, she offered the following: "Let prayerful seduction be your guide." Emma made it clear that the word *prayer* meant beseeching or requesting. She then added that I needed to pay attention to whom or what I am giving the power to confirm my goodness. She continued by saying that I need to ask the seduction to reveal its strength and what might be the best way to return to myself.

Of course, the problem in dealing with seduction is that it feels so good, often accompanied by the lure of grander things. It's like getting an instant shot of unbridled affirmation. The work is to stay focused on the price for the seductive promise. It became clear that the price was my ability to individuate, and when that happens, there's a betrayal of one's soul. We relinquish the quest of simply being who we are meant to be.

I had worked in the simple confines of my basement office, seeing clients without receiving a great deal of fanfare or distinction. Three years ago, a protégé and old friend invited me to join her organization, which offered training and transformational coaching to leaders, most of whom were in Europe. I began receiving requests for coaching sessions and opportunities to teach that reached far beyond my basement.

I began to feel the lure of deciding that these requests and opportunities were obvious declarations of my worth, credibility, and importance. As the invitations increased, I felt bewitched, wondering, "Why not allow these enticements to be testimonials of my greatness?"

Here was the chance to employ the prayerful seduction suggested by Emma. I could see how easy it could be to have these commendations hold power over and responsibility for my value. Why should I have to struggle to remember that I'm okay when someone's desire to benefit from my gifts could do all the work! I could see that it would take some work to subdue the temptation.

I began to ask how the seduction might inform me. The starting point was to be honest about the options: I could either give away the power to confirm my worth or keep it. I then realized that much of the allure had to do with the inventory I was presently taking of my life: Have I given enough? Have I done enough? Have I created enough? Am I enough? How tempting it was to believe that those seeking my services could answer these questions for me.

The price of succumbing to the temptation was becoming more obvious. Giving the power away to confirm my goodness meant being taken hostage by whoever wanted my time and energy. They would define not only my worth but also my life. The seduction also revealed that I would be condemned to show up over and over again, proving I deserved their acclaim and recognition. It also implied that my next delivery better be more impressive than the last. My chest and guts contracted with a feeling of overwhelm draping over my entire body.

I saw the power of the seduction coming more clearly from me. I was teaching people how to care for themselves, and I was being asked to model it as best I could. However, I could also see how the power I gave the seduction served me. It was like lifting weights at the gym. My psyche's muscle strengthened as I felt the weight of the seduction pull me away, then pull back, embracing the task of reclaiming my worth.

I sensed I had achieved some immunity against the seduction's potency. Ironically, the more I acknowledged its power, the greater the strength I attained to resist. Increasingly, the prayerful seduction not only helped me to individuate; it also confirmed my identity as a messenger. Similar to the local mail delivery person, I had messages to deliver. The more I integrated the identity of the messenger, the need to impress softened. I'm not sure how, but the more I felt like a messenger, the more ready I felt to transition. After all, I had delivered lots of messages.

INTERIOR BUCKET LIST

Typically, a bucket list consists of must-see places to visit before the end of one's life. All of which is fine. However, an interior bucket list may be more helpful in support of getting ready to transition. Here are some example interior bucket list items:

- Offer a gift to someone anonymously, allowing the ego's need to be witnessed as generous to wane.

- Offer thanks to someone in your past for what they gave you.
- Make a commitment to meditate more often.
- Do what you need to forgive yourself for that mistake that keeps gnawing at you.
- Call someone you miss and tell them you miss them.
- Pay for the customer behind you in the Starbucks drive-through lane.
- Remember to pause, curious about what is happening around you and in you.

Be creative with your list, individuating how you will transition.

THE GIFT OF A DIMINISHING FUTURE

When you're not trying to get somewhere, you can be here. Aging means you have more history or a past than you do a future. Goals begin to feel a bit silly. They were once a great way to dream. Now, they lose their appeal as there simply may not be enough time to realize them. Besides, by now, you would have learned that your aspirations and intentions would lose their agency as reality would have its way, bringing some blemish to the original dream.

Emma would often say, "The best way to transition or die is to live more, especially with gratitude." Living takes place in the pause and the embrace of stillness. You are living intimately. You and life see each other, with nowhere to go, only to allow yourself to be touched by how much was given to you.

13: DYING

"So many people I worked with died with the grudge of being owed
something by life that they now won't live to collect on. Their deaths
were a theft and betrayal and rip-off for them, and their families
and friends and communities all inherited the poverty,
the stinginess, of that belligerent wound."

– Stephen Jenkinson

After hearing me recite the above passage, Emma squinted her
eyes and said, "Why do you think so many of us die with the
grudge of being owed something by life?"

"I have been giving it some significant consideration—
mostly because I don't want to die that way. My guess is that
If I don't live my heart's love, then I will feel ripped off by life.
Living my heart's love is certainly one expression of a well-
lived life. Living with a future orientation could really have me
feeling ripped off by life since any actual satisfaction can only
happen in the here and now. Getting distraction from what
truly matters can easily lead to a feeling of being ripped off
since I would have forgotten to attend to a lot of the good stuff.
Forgetting to live from a place of gratitude could also have me
feeling like life stole something from me. Gratitude is such a
significant marker of having been well fed by life," I added,
wondering if Emma might have more thoughts on the matter.

"I appreciate your thinking about this idea of dying feeling 'ripped off' by life. I might only add 'living by being risk avoidant.' It's too easy to allow fear to take over a day at a time until there is a large portion of a life unlived due to fear. Life isn't interested in whether we are ready to boldly meet it. Situations, people, and events happen and then gradually fade into the past," offered Emma as her thoughts and my own drifted into the room with an air of satisfying collaboration.

"As I listen to you, I'm wondering if the ripped-off feeling might also arise from an unhealed childhood, where the wounds of emotional deprivation reflected by a lack of affection, love, nurturance, encouragement, acknowledgment, and attention desperately awaited reparation for damages accrued," I suggested, wondering if some part of me might be waiting for such reparations.

"Yes, of course. The ripped-off feeling can also come from an over-identification with life's inherent insecurity and unpredictability. When that happens, the person believes that life's challenges, trials, and ordeals were simply about their life rather than life itself. Rather than responding with curiosity regarding what life may be asking for, they wait for their life to have more ease, more gentleness, and likely, better luck. The waiting can easily extend to their final days, and then they feel ripped off and that life owes them," Emma explained, leaving me wondering how I might avoid the ripped-off feeling at the end of my journey.

"I've been paying attention to what it means to support the transition from being here on the planet to leaving. I have found it a bit challenging to accept how appropriate this preparation is during the winter of my life," I acknowledged, realizing how much I had denied my mortality, allowing the idea of transitioning to receive sparse attention.

"You seemed up to the task of inventorying your regrets. How did you do with the notion of a prayerful seduction?" Emma asked.

"I began to see how beneficial it is to ask for information from the seduction and to see where the call away from myself lives. I also get how much that process supports individuation, which calls for a great deal of humility—an area where I come up a bit short. I appreciated the significance of being touched by wonder resulting from letting go of a demanding inquiry and accepting the journey as deeply mysterious," I revealed, again feeling this nagging reminder that I have an easier time talking about things I haven't yet integrated into real action.

I went on to describe the interior bucket list and the gift provided by a diminishing future. Emma nodded affirmatively and said, "Well, it's time to talk about dying."

"I knew the topic was inevitable, and it's not my favorite," I emphasized, my voice trailing off.

"You know, we're a culture that values strong egos, and strong egos don't accept death as a reality. A strong ego gets attached to the false notion that it is exempt from dying. Plus, you've been dying a lot already," explained Emma with a tone bordering on condescending yet without a hint of reproach.

"I'm not sure what you mean by 'dying a lot already,'" I admitted with no quickening of eagerness igniting within me.

"Your very first act was not to be born but rather to die. You left the safest and most comfortable environment you'll ever know: your mother's womb. Your stay there ended, and it was likely a traumatic ending. We don't customarily talk about endings as a death. We like staying with euphemisms for death," assured Emma, leaving me thankful that at least she sounded like she knew what we were talking about.

"Yeah, I get it; I've been dying a lot. It just seems that taking my last breath is quite a different ending than all the other deaths," I offered, knowing full well how challenging it was for me to hold the faith that, after my last breath, there would be some form of birth.

"The gods will breathe you after you take your last breath," declared Emma, with an extended silence hanging heavily in the room as I waited for her to say more.

"Do you want to say more about the gods doing the breathing?" I asked, hoping to hear some well-developed, cogent account of the afterlife, whether I agreed with it or not.

"No. What I do want to say is that your ego, like all egos, has been pretending that it knows exactly what happens after something ends or dies. You graduated from high school and then college, pretending you knew what would happen next or what marriage would be like. The mystery of endings has us feeling scared and helpless, so we pretend we know what's coming. Of course, when we get ready to physically die, the vastness of the mystery surrounding what's next overwhelms us. We never developed a relationship with a simple truth; we don't know what will happen when something ends, but something will happen," Emma shared, her demeanor communicating more compassion.

"You're right. I have pretended lots of times rather than felt the fear and helplessness, and maybe, I've gotten a bit slipshod addressing the losses that accompany endings," I admitted, beginning to accept that my way of doing it had not been exceptionally unusual.

"Life is about impermanence, impermanence is about change, and change produces loss. In fact, the only guarantee of love is loss. Someone will either die or walk away. A full life asks us to grieve our losses," noted Emma, again weaving her casual manner into the discussion.

"I'm sure you're not saying that we should be constantly shrouded in melancholy, wrapped in deep sorrow," I responded in the hope of securing agreement.

"No, of course, joy must have its place. Grieving lifts heavy sorrow, making room for joy. However, the good times are seductive. We get enthralled with the idea of creating a life of pleasure, excitement, and ease. We trick ourselves into believing that a life stripped of sorrow, grief, and loss is a good life. We need to gently bring ourselves back to the truth that life is much about loss, and that grief is what allows us to both honor what is lost and prepare for what life will bring next," continued Emma, impressing me about how much elderhood depends on getting over the ego's notion of the "good life."

She suggested I read *The Wild Edge of Sorrow* by Francis Weller. It didn't take long before I could appreciate the wisdom of Weller and have more understanding of Emma's thoughts about grief. He writes: "It is the accumulated losses of a lifetime that slowly weigh us down—the times of rejection, the moments of isolation when we felt cut off from the sustaining touch of comfort and love. It is an ache that resides in the heart, the faint echo calling us back to times of loss. We are called back, not so much to make things right but to acknowledge what happened to us. Grief asks that we honor the loss and, in doing so, deepen our capacity for compassion."

I returned to Emma's with excitement about Weller's suggestion that grief has us honoring the losses, which deepens our capacity for compassion. Emma and I spoke of the immense opportunity life offers us for both psychological and physical losses. We also focused on the losses that occur when a dream ends. It makes sense to see that when a relationship ends, the dream accompanying that relationship also ends. We may carry dreams of trips, creating a home, growing old together, creating friendships, celebrating holidays and special events, offerings of a warm body on a cold winter night, or sharing mutual support in the face of life's demands. Relationships have a history, a present, and at least a dream of a future.

I left Emma's bearing her encouragement to explore the honoring issued by grief and the deepening of our ability to be compassionate. I was stepping onto new ground with fear and the hope that my ego could step aside, allowing me to metabolize this thinking about honoring loss.

HONORING AND DEEPENING

An old way to understand the word *honoring* is as "deep re-spect," and as pointed out earlier, the word *respect* means "de-serving to be regarded and acknowledged." When grief is hon-ored, we can hear the voices of grief, voices amplified by the heart: "Life has lost its meaning." "My heart is broken beyond repair." "I no longer know what is important." "Joy comes to an end." "I only know the depths of emptiness." "Love has for-saken me." "The gods have betrayed me." "I am truly lost and do not know my way."

These voices offer honor to what or who is lost. The place of the loss is held in reverence for how much importance was bestowed upon our lives. The voices give testimony to the hol-lowness left behind. Loss and grief represent a place where we truly know one another. Here, we are no longer strangers. We know what it means to have the object of our love and devo-tion removed. We understand that we are no longer the per-son we were before the loss. Our hearts carry a heavier beat yet with a softer tone.

We think differently; our bodies move more slowly, no longer driven by overt and nuanced anticipations of the be-loved. We struggle to hold a meaningful vision of the future with the weight of absence upon us. Even the image facing us in the mirror appears somewhat alien. We simply do not know who we are. The truth is that we are dying as someone's spouse, someone's child, someone's parent, someone's friend or colleague.

When we grieve consciously and accept that grief will have its way with us, we can see the other as a fellow pilgrim on a perilous journey. Compassion, or the ability to feel into the other's sorrow, comes with more ease. Dynamics of competi-tion and hierarchy are eliminated, replaced by "I know you in the depths of your loss, and I can join you there." Petty efforts aimed at separation wash away as I allow myself to welcome my grief. I have come to understand humanity.

HEALING

Emma and I had been meeting for six years. She not only spoke of what a soulful path to elderhood looked like; she modeled it. I was pleased to see that the sexism I held when we first met had considerably lessened, with our gender difference having little or no impact on my understanding of elderhood. Our next conversation, like so many others, surprised me and fed me well.

"You seem to be clear about the honoring provided by grief and the ensuing compassion," noted Emma, her cheeks and gaze softening.

"That's right. I appreciate how much loss connects us all. Loss loses its capacity to connect us when someone is running as fast as possible in order not to feel it," I added, knowing I was not above running.

"I'm wondering how well you're holding the role of healing in the process of bringing grace to the dying experience. And, of course, grace becomes possible when we make peace with aging and dying," said Emma with palpable curiosity.

"While talking to my friend Ray the other day, I realized how much he desires peace. He described being aware of every moment evaporating into the next and the next. There was something about holding a deep, felt sense of peace for him. I knew that there was some healing needed for me to both desire and know peace," I offered, feeling a longing for such peace with a slight hint of fear in my belly.

"I sense a good deal of melancholy in your voice," responded Emma.

"Yes, I feel forlorn as I wonder what I do rather than seek

peace," I puzzled, knowing that the alternative to peace would shortly be disclosed.

"Well, what do you do rather than seek peace?" inquired Emma with a knowing eye.

"I'm not necessarily proud of what I do. I tend to get caught up in demonstrating something, proving, competing, and striving," I confided, knowing that these endeavors not only fell quite short of me seeking peace but, in some unidentified way, also hurt me.

"Okay, those pursuits are what you have been moving toward. However, is there anything you've been moving away from?" Emma asked, the question touching me as an invitation I felt ambivalent about accepting.

"I have noticed some strong reactions lately when I experience a friend being significantly externally referenced," I explained, knowing there was some form of agitation about to be revealed.

"By 'externally referenced,' I assume you mean seeing a friend's attention strongly driven toward the external world rather than the interior world. And, given your strong reaction, I can assume it reminds you of something that lives close to you," Emma added, her wisdom once again calling me to myself.

"I mean, I'm seventy-three and have been working on myself for over three decades! How many times do I need to look back toward where I come from?" I exclaimed, expecting some other result than the one at hand, which angered me.

"We look back as many times as we need to look forward. There's no other way to release ourselves from the grip of the past. We are either addressing the past, or the past is addressing us. The latter tends to be a bit more challenging, as you know," Emma explained, reminding me of an old truth that I had allowed to escape me.

"But what does looking back have to do with getting ready

to die?" I questioned, knowing that somehow it did.

"It's not just about looking back. It's about bringing healing to what's back there. An old meaning of the word *medicine* is 'to embellish.' We bring medicine to our suffering by increasing our attention to the injury, bringing more curiosity, more emotion, more of a regulated nervous system, and more compassion for ourselves and the perpetrators—all that never happens by making only one or two trips back there," explained Emma, feeling both the rightness of her words and how much my ego was attached to landing in some honorable destination.

As I listened to her words, images of my mother's devotion to people, places, and mostly things paraded across my mind's eye. My childhood was inundated with countless maternal mandates to ignore my interior world. Ideas, imagination, intuition, and emotion were all relegated to a category identified as a waste of time. I went on to describe to Emma the anger and hurt created by that experience.

"I know you've paid attention to your maternal wound as well as your father, who colluded with her delusion. What I want you to notice now is how much you've compensated by being driven to acknowledge and express your interior world. You spend a great deal of time in reflection. You teach and write from that world. You're a healer who calls people to their inner worlds. My God, you taught philosophy, which is a major call to the mind. All these endeavors are fine, but when they are driven by having to prove that someone in your past was wrong, they lose a significant measure of soul," offered Emma, bringing an unavoidable illumination to how much I was caught up in compensating for my mother's orientation.

"I see the loss of soul in the story, which may be asking for a particular medicine. My hunch is to embellish the story by acknowledging the likelihood of shame and fear haunting my mother's inner world. I am more able to hold the woundedness of both my parents and loosen my grip on the illusion of deserving a more sanitized childhood," I added, feeling my heart open to accepting that my parents did the best they could, and that it wasn't enough for me.

"I respect that. You sound like you're able to hold the depth of the injury you experienced as well as the depth of injury experienced by your parents. You're now honoring both you and them. The gift you offer yourself is that nothing toxic like resentment, blame, or disdain holds you captive in your past. It is a wonderful preparation for dying," explained Emma, her words holding themselves in the room as if to give me the opportunity to be with them.

"I appreciate your acknowledgment, and it is important for me to say that I had to go back to the past many times with resentment and anger before what you call the more toxic elements dissipated. It's been an arduous journey. I want to write a blessing for my father's unlived dreams and the son who so wanted to live his dreams for him," I offered with a sigh of relief.

Emma simply nodded gracefully. As I left her that day, I felt a burdensome weight lifted by the possibility of my being more open to welcoming peace.

BLESSINGS FOR DREAMS LIVED AND UNLIVED

I watched you with eyes of the heart. You sat alone in the den in that old beige chair, next to which a dim lamp appeared to struggle to shed enough light for reading. You sat night after night, your glasses tipped forward onto your nose, eyes peering down into an encyclopedia's version of history. Ancient times filled your heart, but there would be no books or education to bring a genuine historian into being. No, tethering patterns from the past would hold you to something much smaller. Your dream to take your place among those who would give voice to the human story would go unlived.

You knew how to tell a story. Moments after you began to speak, the bodies of the listeners would resonate with your words. It never felt like one man telling some narrative as eros filled the room with an enchantment escorting everyone somewhere they had never been before. Everyone's eyes were enlarged with both gratitude and welcome for your story. You possessed the calling to be able to live in a story, and everyone knew it. What I never quite understood was why the same anticipation existed in your audience even when they were about to hear a story they had heard before. What allowed you to transcend the ennui of redundancy?

The image of you with your encyclopedia in hand, sitting under dim light, was burned into my soul. How could I save my father from the unlived life of his dreams? How could I save myself? I desperately convinced myself that I could live the dreams of two men. I look back now, in the winter of my life, and wonder, what was my dream? How could I know my dream from some borrowed sentiment? Maybe now, dreams that preferred to be hidden dare to show themselves.

I close my eyes now and allow for a blend of honesty laced with enchantment to shape an image of a boy taking his father's hand as an encyclopedia falls gently in his lap. "Come with me. I will live our dreams for the both of us."

That boy's manhood would be challenged to hold some measure of having done enough, of feeling he was enough. The voice of limitless striving was always close by, reminding him of his father's unlived dreams. Never quite knowing when my dream had taken a full breath as the unlived in my father beckoned me.

Two unwelcome gifts have helped me move closer to what is being asked of me: a pandemic and a suite of Ménière's symptoms. The combination has brought helplessness,

ɛrability, and a pause that has my body regularly shedding
ion. Has this tension been separating me from the voice of
my soul? Or has it been the tremor hurrying me to the next
moment where I hope to live enough dreams for two men?
Could there be in every pause a quiet but salient welcome?

In this pause, there is an image cradled in active imagination. I'm standing at that chair, the one dimly lit with my father in his khaki trousers and a green-and-black flannel shirt.
He holds my hand and says, "I want you to let go now, Paulie.
Do not look harshly upon these unlived dreams of mine, mine
to embrace and feel, and I'm the one who must listen to their
voices. Unlived dreams are not simply a source of defeat. They
can reveal unyielding fear and the narratives, making it courageous to long for something larger. Unlived dreams are
awaiting insemination from the spirit. You have loved me
dearly, and I ask you to love me now by allowing your limits
to embrace your own dreams.

"I, as well as our ancestors, rest easy as you cease pushing
life, allowing life to hold you the way it was always meant to
hold you. Come to know this holding. You will never find it in
busy, for busy has you stepping just beyond life's enfolding
immediacy. Move slowly, holding the faith that in the pause,
an intimacy with life will be consummated.

"In each pause, find repose in your body. Only then will you
be available to receive life gently revealing its mystery. You will
no longer need to dismiss some subtle expression of the sub-
lime. Life always had a dream that it wanted to live in you."

A BLESSING FOR PEACE

I simply thought you were unapproachable,
and certainly unattainable.
I never imagined that I was choosing to avoid you;
it's just that there seemed to be so many other deserving endeavors.

It wasn't until I paused, watching a friend invite peace,
that I realized I was responsible for the state of our relationship.

I pretended to know you as friends do
referring to each other by a nickname.
I called you serenity, equanimity, tranquility,
composure, and centeredness.
All pretense for actual estrangement.
It was plain to see I looked my best,
like an admirer feigning a connection to a celebrity.

I'm certainly more available now,
wondering how I might get to know you.
I at least believe you are worth getting to know.
I must admit that I don't know your gifts.
I can extend a welcome to you
as I admit being taken hostage by a voice from the past
that called me away from myself.

Only then could I understand my strivings to prove
I was someone other than who I was told I should be.
How many times must a man cry out,
"This is who I am!"
before he hears his voice.
This crying out has exhausted me and brought me here.
This fatigue offers an endearing welcome to a peaceful man.

I thought being a peacemaker meant bringing some
measure of armistice to the outside world.
I see now that being a peacemaker means knowing how to bring
peace to my breath and heartbeat.
Peace comes in the suspension of hostilities
created by a demand to prove something.
Proving is now laid to rest.

SACRED AND SACRED

"How have you been doing welcoming peace into your life?" asked Emma, while I remembered that without more peace, I could be a dying, ripped-off person.

"I have been giving it some significant consideration. Mostly because I don't want to die feeling that life owes me. My guess is that if I don't live my heart's love, then I will feel ripped off by life. Living my heart's love is certainly one expression of a well-lived life. Living with a future orientation could have me feeling ripped off by life since any real satisfaction can only happen in the here and now. Getting distracted from what truly matters can easily lead to a feeling of being ripped off since I would have forgotten to attend to a lot of the good stuff.

"I'm reminded of the words of my friend Jim, who asks, 'For what do you need to seize permission to live your soul's desire?' I'm thinking that it's peace. I have not prioritized peace, and it's time," I asserted, feeling more permission to allow myself to live with serenity.

"You seem to be more receptive to bringing and allowing peace in your life. What are you learning?" inquired Emma, her tone suggesting I would indeed take on the task of learning.

"For sure, I'm aware on a deeper level that I've been rushing off to the next moment to prove something, if only to prove that I am different from the vision my parents held regarding who I should be. I certainly pushed peace out of the way to get there. It does feel strange at seventy-three to be up to the business of demonstrating that I'm okay despite not being who my parents wanted me to be," I shared, somewhat embarrassed and feeling more accepting that my embarrassment may simply be an indication of me slowly mitigating my vanity.

"Not strange at all! It's what we've been speaking about.

The soulful path is about continuing to relinquish some borrowed ethos, and in doing so, you animate your individuation. But let's get back to what you're learning about allowing yourself to be touched by peace," Emma encouraged, leaning forward, suggesting there was much for me to understand about living with more peace.

"I can see that my fatigue is asking for peace and that peace offers me a much-needed renewal," I responded, confident that Emma would expand upon my understanding.

"Yes, for sure, renewal is one of the gifts provided by peace. One key to allowing both your mind and your body to experience peace. The more you nurture yourself, the more peace finds openings to enter your life. Play more, nap more, watch simple television programs, read novels, express your sense of humor, tell wild and outlandish stories, and spend time with your dog," Emma instructed, the light in her eyes suggesting her investment in me accruing these benefits.

"I get how spacious nurturing can be, offering an invitation to peace. Actually, just talking about it makes me feel peaceful," I added.

"The more you decline with age, the more nurturing you need and deserve. The closer you get to death, the less you can protest the loss of strength and gain more peace. Let me read this brief passage from *The Grace of Dying* by Kathleen Dowling Singh: 'In the Nearing Death Experience, clinging and resistance end with sustained weakness and with grace. With the end of clinging and resistance, with grace, comes peace: the experience of empty mind, open heart.'"

"I'm touched by her words. I'm assuming we can always practice interrupting the habits of clinging and resisting along the way," I responded, aware that I was hearing what gets in my way when regarding genuine surrender.

"Sure, you can. The nearing-death experience simply amplifies the opportunity. One way to look at this is to suggest that the gifts of peace become more obvious as you allow aging to touch you without clinging to what you're being asked to sacrifice. I mean, aging is an extremely sacred and sacred time," Emma offered, not concealing how satisfied she felt saying something that made almost no sense to me.

"Okay, so what does 'sacred and sacred' mean?"

"Well, you know the two ancient definitions of the word *sacred.*"

"Yes, I do. One definition is 'confirming what truly matters,' and the other is 'to sacrifice,'" I responded, not sure where she planned to take this.

"That's right. Confirming what truly matters and sacrificing describe the soulful path of elderhood. They are what potentially makes old age so sacred. We're asked to sacrifice so much that we naturally cling to, things like how we look, what we achieve, how strong and agile we are, how much recognition we are receiving, how effectively we can market ourselves, how many material possessions we can acquire, driving an impressive automobile, making sure our lawns are properly manicured, and confirming our connection to people in high places. The willingness to make such sacrifices creates a stillness and a peace, and in that peace, we can continue to confirm what truly matters," explained Emma with characteristic softness.

"I'm hearing that being willing to sacrifice or stop clinging is the key to confirming what truly matters. I also see how the two definitions of the word *sacred* work together, 'sacred and sacred,' as you say. It does imply that we spend much of our lives confirming what doesn't really matter. Isn't that an unfortunate waste of time?" I wondered, knowing that Emma would find a meaningful place for what I defined as a waste of time.

"No, not at all. The ego must have its day in the sun, driven by vanity, greed, arrogance, grandiosity, and delusion. If you could immediately confirm what truly matters when you turn eighteen, then there would be no reason to come here and allow life to deepen you and forge some significant personal development. You might as well remain wherever you were before you came here," Emma added, with a large belly laugh I hadn't quite ever seen the likes of.

"I guess that's what it means to stumble toward enlightenment. I get how much sacrificing allows us to confirm what truly matters," I suggested.

"That's right. Sacrifice brings us back to ourselves. It backs us up toward ourselves. That's why I've encouraged you to be careful about the amount of protest you issue when life asks you to sacrifice. When you allow the sacrifice to back you up in yourself, you find stillness and peace there. From that peace, distractions fall away, and you are granted more clarity regarding what truly matters. You live with less distortion, embraced by the sacred and the sacred," Emma explained, her tone possessing an assurance that we may have explored the depths of a soulful path to elderhood.

"I'm getting that peace isn't simply a comforting feeling. It sounds like the gateway to what is truly sacred, what truly matters," I offered, feeling the tone of my attitude toward aging losing its victim's voice.

When the pandemic came, Emma and I met virtually. It took us a while to get the technology straight, and I didn't cling to a need to be highly competent at it. After all, people our age didn't grow up with technology except for a landline phone, a transistor radio, and a television.

"I came across a poem that highlighted so much of what we have been exploring about aging, and I want to read it to you. It's entitled 'At Peace,' by Amado Nervo."

"I'd love to hear it," Emma invited.

AT PEACE

Very near my setting sun, I bless you, Life
because you never gave me neither unfilled hope
nor unfair work, nor undeserved sorrow/pain

because I see at the end of my rough way
that I was the architect of my own destiny
and if I extracted the sweetness or the bitterness of things
it was because I put the sweetness or the bitterness in them
when I planted rose bushes I always harvested roses

Certainly, winter is going to follow my youth
But you didn't tell me that May was eternal
I found without a doubt long my nights of pain
But you didn't promise me only good nights
And, in exchange, I had some peaceful ones.

I loved, I was loved, the sun caressed my face

Life, you owe me nothing, Life, we are at peace!

As I looked up toward the computer screen, wondering whether the poem might have touched Emma, I saw her eyes closed with gentle streams of tears falling from her cheeks. I wanted her to know that the poem had become my anthem for the soulful path to elderhood and that the phrases "Life, you owe me nothing, Life, we are at peace!" and "I dearly hope I have served you well" had become the mantras for my aging soul. Instead, I simply joined her, our tears feeling like a prayer of thanks for our days together.

Emma continues to be an *anam cara*, or soul friend. She calls to my attention what is less than complimentary as well as what is praiseworthy within me. She no longer needs to remind me that soulful elderhood is not a place I'm destined to arrive. I walk the path, often stumbling, allured by some invitation to my vanity or an illusion of power. I do spend less time wandering aimlessly away from the path, with many thanks to Emma.

REFERENCES

Chapter One

Thich Nhat Hanh. "Thay's Poetry / Please Call Me by My True Names (Song & Poem)." 2020. Plum Village. June 3, 2020. https://plumvillage.org/articles/please-call-me-by-my-true-names-song-poem/.

Ellison, Ralph. (1952) 2018. Invisible Man. Brantford, Ontario: W. Ross Macdonald School Resource Services Library.

Sartre, Jean Paul. 1945. Le Flore. "There is no traced out path to lead man to his salvation; he must constantly invent his own path. But, to invent it he is free, responsible, without excuse, and every hope lies within him."

Weller, Francis. "Rough Initiations." March 4, 2021. Kosmos Journal. Accessed June 17, 2021.

Chapter Two

Hollis, James. 1993. The Middle Passage: From Misery to Meaning in Midlife. Toronto. Inner City Books.

Weller, Francis. Winter 2021 "Rough Initiations." Kosmos Journal. Accessed March 4, 2021.

Chapter Three

Socrates. 2011. "Beware the Barrenness of a Busy Life." Philosiblog.com. April 11, 2011.

Chapter Four

The Legend of Bagger Vance. Directed by Jeremy Leven, Dreamworks, 2000.

Moore, Thomas. 2000. Original Self: Living with Paradox and Authenticity. New York: HarperCollins.

Chapter Six

Frost, Robert. 1923. New Hampshire. Henry Holt.

Chapter Seven

Hollis, James. 2018. Living an Examined Life: Wisdom for the Second Half of the Journey. Boulder, Colorado. Sounds True.

Van Der Kolk, Bessel. 2014. The Body Keeps the Score: Brain, Mind, and Body in the Healing of Trauma. New York, New York. Penguin Books

Rainer Maria Rilke, Franz Xaver Kappus, and Reginald Snell. 2002. Letters to a Young Poet. Mineola, N.Y. Dover Publications.

Levine, Peter A. 2010. In an Unspoken Voice: How the Body Releases Trauma and Restores Goodness. Berkeley, California. North Atlantic Books.

Barks, Coleman. 1995. The Essential Rumi. New York. Castle Books.

Chapter Eight

"The Art of Being Wise Is Knowing What to Overlook." 2018. *Families of Character* (blog). September 26, 2018.

"Henry David Thoreau Philosophy Summary" in Philosophy & Philosophers, August 21, 2019.

May, Rollo. 1994. The Courage to Create. New York; London. W. W. Norton & Company.

Chapter Nine

Emerson, Ralph Waldo, and University of California Libraries. 1836. Nature. Internet Archive. Boston. James Munroe and Company.

Charles Dickens, Georgina Hogarth, Mamie Dickens, Laurence Hutton, Richard Herne Shepherd. 1908. "Letters and Speeches".

Niebuhr, Reinhold. 1943. "The Serenity Prayer." Tag line to a sermon.

Chapter Ten

Reporter, Excellence. 2020. "Carl Jung: On the Wisdom and the Meaning of Life." Excellence Reporter. January 6, 2020.

Rainer Maria Rilke, Franz Xaver Kappus, and Reginald Snell. 2002. Letters to a Young Poet. Mineola, N.Y. Dover Publications.

Chapter Eleven

Hollis, James. 2018. Living an Examined Life: Wisdom for the Second Half of the Journey. Boulder, Colorado. Sounds True.

O'Donohue, John. 2008. To Bless the Space between Us: A Book of Blessings. New York: Doubleday.

Keats, John. Letter to George Keats & Georgiana Keats. April 21, 1819.

Chapter Twelve

Luke, Helen M. 1987. Old Age: Journey Into Simplicity. New York. Bell Tower.

Dowling Singh, Kathleen. 2000. The Grace in Dying: How We Are Transformed Spiritually as We Die. San Francisco. Harper One.

Campbell, Joseph, and Diane K Osbon. 1998. A Joseph Campbell Companion: Reflections on the Art of Living. New York, New York. Harper Perennial.

Chapter Thirteen

Jenkinson, Stephen. 2015. Die Wise: A Manifesto for Sanity and Soul. Berkeley, California. North Atlantic Books.

Weller, Francis. 2015. The Wild Edge of Sorrow. North Atlantic Books, U.S.

Dowling Singh, Kathleen. 2000. The Grace in Dying: How We Are Transformed Spiritually as We Die. San Francisco. Harper One.

Nervo, Amado. n.d. "At Peace by Amado Ruiz de Nervo." Allpoetry.com. Accessed April 17, 2020.

PERMISSIONS

Prologue

Meade, Michael, author of "Fate and Destiny: The Two Agreements of the Soul".

Chapter One

From Eternal Echoes by John O'Donohue. Copyright(c) 1999 by John O'Donohue. Used by permission of HarperCollins Publishers.

Chapter Two

Meade, Michael, author of "Men and the Water of Life: Initiation and the Tempering of Men".

Chapter Five

Excerpt(s) from BECOMING WISE: AN INQUIRY INTO THE MYSTERY AND ART OF LIVING by Krista Tippett, copyright © 2016 by Krista Tippett. Used by permission of Penguin Press, an imprint of Penguin Publishing Group, a division of Penguin Random House LLC. All rights reserved.

Meade, Michael, author of "Awakening the Soul: A Deep Response to a Troubled World".

Meade, Michael, author of "Awakening the Soul: A Deep Response to a Troubled World".

Chapter Seven

Frankl, Viktor E, Ilse Lasch, Harold S Kushner, and William J Winslade. 2006. Man's Search for Meaning. Boston. Beacon Press.

Chapter Eight

Meade, Michael, author of "Fate and Destiny: The Two Agreements of the Soul".

Chapter Nine

Excerpt(s) from 12 RULES FOR LIFE: AN ANTIDOTE TO CHAOS by Jordan Peterson, Copyright © 2018 Luminate Psychological Services, Ltd. Reprinted by permission of Random House Canada, a division of Random House Canada Limited. All rights reserved.

Chapter Twelve

Gawande, Atul. 2015. *Being Mortal: Medicine and What Matters in the End.* New York, N.Y. Picador.

Thorough efforts have been made to secure all permissions. Any omissions or corrections will be made in future editions.

ACKNOWLEDGMENTS

I have been immensely fortunate to have been mentored through the years by John Julian, Henri Nouwen, Ray Walker, George Rogers, Alfred Alschuler, James Hollis, and Norcott Pemberton. Their guidance interrupted my varying inclinations to meander where I likely did not belong. They mentored me with unparalleled integrity yielding regular reminders that the truth I was seeking lay within me. Their devotion allowed me to return to a path holding the potential of my elderhood.

Special thanks to James Hollis for championing my writing, leaving me with greater faith in my ability to bring more meaning to aging. I am especially grateful for Jim's aging being a harbinger of how I might also serve from my elderhood. His devotion to service and ability to hold on to what truly matters in life leave me considerably more welcoming of my years. For sure, Jim has brought a warm light to the winter of my life.

I have been blessed with friends and colleagues who want to know me and be known by me. This mutual investment continues to be the bedrock of what it means for me to belong. The group includes Amy Fox, Hilorie Baer, Andi Borman, Jen Cohen, Ester Martinez, Martin Boroson, Nancy Hyatt, Karyn Saganic, Michael Paprocki, Thom Allena, Gary Blaser, Ray Di Capua, Marie Pace, Deirdre O'Connor, and Wendy Shami.

I am also extremely blessed to have served committed protegees including Margaret Harris, Peter Drake, Jody Grose, and Jennifer Jondreau Thompson. Each of whom has taken some vision of mine and allowed their discriminating thinking and intuition to reflect their uniqueness as practitioners.

Many thanks to Amy Mercury for gathering supporting materials, managing details, and making the manuscript ready for Atmosphere Press.

Also, gratitude to my editor, BE Allatt, who brought a rigorous eye to sentence structure as well as modifying language to be reader-friendly.

Lastly, I am deeply grateful for my wife Connie Jones Dunion, who continues to join me in this apprenticeship in emotional intimacy. Our relationship calls to the fool within me who helps mitigate my contrived certainty related to love and intimacy. Thus, allowing me to return to appreciation for warm gazes and touch, simple acts of kindness, and honesty accompanied by compassion. How lucky I am to grow old with such a lover and companion.

ABOUT ATMOSPHERE PRESS

Atmosphere Press is an independent, full-service publisher for excellent books in all genres and for all audiences. Learn more about what we do at atmospherepress.com.

We encourage you to check out some of Atmosphere's latest releases, which are available at Amazon.com and via order from your local bookstore:

Finding Us, by Kristin Rehkamp
The Ideological and Political System of Banselism, by Royard Halmonet Vantion (Ancheng Wang)
Unconditional: Loving and Losing an Addict, by Lizzy and Adam
Telling Tales and Sharing Secrets, by Jackie Collins, Diana Kinared, and Sally Showalter
Nursing Homes: A Missionary's Journey Through Heaven's Waiting Room, by Tim Eatman Ph.D.
Timeline of Stars, by Joe Adcock
A Boy Who Loved Me, by Wilson Semitti
The Injustice in Justice, by Charmaine Loverin
Living in the Gray, by Katie Weber
Living with Veracity, Dying with Dignity, by Alison Clay-Duboff
Noah's Rejects, by Rob Kagan
A lot of Questions (with no answers)?, by Jordan Neben
Cowboy from Prague: An Immigrant's Pursuit of the American Dream, by Charles Ota Heller
Sleeping Under the Bridge, by Melissa Baker
The Only Prayer I Ever Have to Say Is Thank You, by M. Kaya Hill
Amygdala Blue, by Paul Lomax
A Caregiver's Love Story, by Nancie Wiseman Attwater
Taming Infection: The American Response to Illness from Smallpox to Covid, by Gregg Coodley and David Sarasohn
The Second Long March, by Patti Isaacs
Me & Mrs. Jones, by Justine Gladden
Echoes from Wuhan, by Gretchen Dykstra

ABOUT THE AUTHOR

 **PAUL DUNION, EdD**, is a teacher, author, and psychological healer committed to remaining mindful of life as a mysterious and unpredictable journey. A steadfast believer in the power of community, Paul founded *Boys to Men,* a mentoring program for teenage boys, and COMEGA, the semi-annual Connecticut Men's Gathering now in its 30th year of service. Paul currently is a Senior Faculty with Mobius Executive Leadership and teaches at Mobius' Next Practice Institute. Storytelling, facilitating, and writing are some of Paul's strongest gifts. He regularly contributes to various online platforms. *My Days with Emma: A Soulful Path to Elderhood*, is his seventh book. Paul lives in eastern Connecticut with his wife, Connie, and dog, Kody.

Made in USA - North Chelmsford, MA
1345735_9781639885718
12.13.2022 1457

.